Christian Logic Puzzles

SIXTY-SIX PUZZLES TO GROW YOUR FAITH

HEATHER MARIE WALKER

WESTBOW
PRESS®
A DIVISION OF THOMAS NELSON
& ZONDERVAN

THE HOLY BIBLE, NEW INTERNATIONAL VERSION®, NIV® Copyright © 1973, 1978, 1984, 2011 by Biblica, Inc.® Used by permission. All rights reserved worldwide.

WestBow Press books may be ordered through booksellers or by contacting:

WestBow Press
A Division of Thomas Nelson & Zondervan
1663 Liberty Drive
Bloomington, IN 47403
www.westbowpress.com
1 (866) 928-1240

Because of the dynamic nature of the Internet, any web addresses or links contained in this book may have changed since publication and may no longer be valid. The views expressed in this work are solely those of the author and do not necessarily reflect the views of the publisher, and the publisher hereby disclaims any responsibility for them.

Any people depicted in stock imagery provided by Thinkstock are models, and such images are being used for illustrative purposes only. Certain stock imagery © Thinkstock.

ISBN: 978-1-9736-0701-4 (sc)
ISBN: 978-1-9736-0702-1 (e)

Library of Congress Control Number: 2017915720

Print information available on the last page.

WestBow Press rev. date: 10/24/2017

In memory of Mrs. Shea, my fourth-grade teacher, who believed that I would write a book someday.

A special thanks to:

The staff and students at Columbia College in Columbia, South Carolina. My stay with you
did not make me the young woman I wanted to be; instead, I became much more.

The staff and students at the Lutheran Theological Southern Seminary,
for here my faith was tested and my knowledge expanded.

The people at Redeemer Lutheran Church in St. Paul, Minnesota; St. Luke's Evangelical Lutheran
Church in Summerville, South Carolina; and College Place United Methodist Church in Columbia,
South Carolina. In these churches, my faith grew among people who cared about me.

Brittany Higgins, my friend and roommate, who put up with me while I wrote this book.

Elmyra, my beautiful cat. She spent almost as much time on my keyboard as I did.

Why Write Christian-Themed Logic Puzzles?

Greetings reader,

I chose to write Christian-themed logic puzzles for four reasons:

First, you should know that there is a God who loves you. Maybe you believe in a loving God; maybe you don't. Regardless, God loves you anyway. This all-powerful, all-knowing, ever-present, unchanging, eternal being created the world and everything in it. When the first humans sinned, all humanity was separated from God and doomed to suffer from brokenness. God was not going to let humanity stay like that. He came down to earth as a baby named Jesus, who would grow up to die on the cross, rise from the dead after three days, and ascend into the sky with the promise of returning. We need to be ready for his return.

Second, I wanted to challenge Christian stereotypes. The way society tends to show Christians in movies and books usually evokes words like "hypocritical," "dishonest," "uncaring," and "power hungry." I am trying to offer a more accurate view of Christians. By the end of this book, some of the words you use to describe Christians will hopefully be "God-seeking," "serving," "loving," "imperfect, but not evil," and "struggling, but not hopeless." These logic puzzles show some of the things that Christians believe and do, both in the church building and in the world.

Third, this is a chance for teaching. It is too easy to call oneself a Christian without knowing what a Christian believes. Does the word "confirmation" confuse you? Can you tell me who Job is? How about Cyrus the Great? Do you know why the Ten Commandments are important? Here is a hint: the Ten Commandments are more than a set of rules. If a non-Christian asked about a biblical concept (such as the Trinity, the Armor of God, grace), could you explain it to that person? These logic puzzles will help you to learn a lot more about Christianity. You shouldn't say that you are a Christian, if you do not understand what a Christian believes.

Fourth, this is a chance to personalize your faith. As people grow from children to adults, they tend to accept the beliefs and values of their parents, teachers, friends, and celebrities. We accept their beliefs by default rather than making them our own. In this way, faith is more like an outfit; it can be taken on and off. Genuine faith can be stretched, wadded, crushed, and obliterated, but it should not be removed as easily as a piece of clothing.

How to Solve the Logic Puzzles

This book is a series of puzzles. The goal is to correctly match up all of the information in each of the puzzles. Clues are given to figure out the who, what, where, when, why, and how questions of each puzzle. I suggest using the grids to solve the puzzles; it's easier that way. I prefer making the boxes with a "y" for "yes" and an "n" for "no." You may check your answers in the answer key at the end of the book. Puzzles are marked as easy, medium, or hard for your convenience.

There are many different types of logic puzzle clues:

"Is" and "Is not" clues. These clues say that something "is" or "is not" true.
For example:
"The runner who completed the race in 25 minutes was sponsored by Dash Co."

Go under the column for 25 minutes and mark the box for Dash Co. with a "y" Likewise, the boxes for Run Co. should be marked with an "n."

"Andy is not the runner who completed the race in 15 minutes."
Follow the row for Andy across the grid and put an "n" in the box for 15 minutes.

		Time to Complete Race					Sponsor (fake companies)				
		5 Minutes	10 Minutes	15 Minutes	20 Minutes	25 Minutes	Dash Co.	Dash Co.	Run Co.	Run Co.	Run Co.
Runner Name	Andy			n							
	Billy										
	Cindy										
	Darcy										
	Ebony										
Sponsor (fake companies)	Dash Co.					y					
	Dash Co.					y					
	Run Co.					n					
	Run Co.					n					
	Run Co.					n					

"And" clues. These are clues where all of the information "is" or "is not" true.
For example:
"Darcy completed the race in 15 minutes and was sponsored by Run Co."

Follow the row for Darcy across the grid. Mark the boxes for 15 minutes and Run Co. with a "y." Mark all other times and sponsors in Darcy's row with an "n." Also, follow the column for 15 minutes down and mark the Run Co. box with a "y." Don't forget to put "n" in the box for Dash Co. at 15 minutes.

		Time to Complete Race					Sponsor (fake companies)				
		5 Minutes	10 Minutes	15 Minutes	20 Minutes	25 Minutes	Dash Co.	Dash Co.	Run Co.	Run Co.	Run Co.
Runner Name	Andy			n							
	Billy			n							
	Cindy			n							
	Darcy	n	n	y	n	n	n	n	y	y	y
	Ebony			n							
Sponsor (fake companies)	Dash Co.			n		y					
	Dash Co.			n		y					
	Run Co.			y		n					
	Run Co.			y		n					
	Run Co.			y		n					

"But" clues. These are clues where part of the information "is" true and part of the information "is not" true. For example:

"Cindy was sponsored by Run Co, but she did not finish the race in 20 minutes."

Follow the row for Cindy across. Mark the Run Co. box with a "y," but mark the 20-minute box with an "n."

		Time to Complete Race					Sponsor (fake companies)				
		5 Minutes	10 Minutes	15 Minutes	20 Minutes	25 Minutes	Dash Co.	Dash Co.	Run Co.	Run Co.	Run Co.
Runner Name	Andy			n							
	Billy			n							
	Cindy			n	n		n	n	y	y	y
	Darcy	n	n	y	n	n	n	n	y	y	y
	Ebony			n							
Sponsor (fake companies)	Dash Co.			n		y					
	Dash Co.			n		y					
	Run Co.			y		n					
	Run Co.			y		n					
	Run Co.			y		n					

"Or" clues. This is a clue where one or more parts of the clue "are not" true. Other clues will be needed to help this clue make sense.
For example:
"Ebony finished the race in 10 or 25 minutes."

Follow the Ebony row across. Mark all time boxes with an "n," except for 10 and 25 minutes. Leave those boxes blank.

		Time to Complete Race					Sponsor (fake companies)				
		5 Minutes	10 Minutes	15 Minutes	20 Minutes	25 Minutes	Dash Co.	Dash Co.	Run Co.	Run Co.	Run Co.
Runner Name	Andy			n							
	Billy			n							
	Cindy			n	n		n	n	y	y	y
	Darcy	n	n	y	n	n	n	n	y	y	y
	Ebony	n		n	n						
Sponsor (fake companies)	Dash Co.			n		y					
	Dash Co.			n		y					
	Run Co.			y		n					
	Run Co.			y		n					
	Run Co.			y		n					

"If, then" statements. These clues can be broken up into two parts (a and b). In these puzzles, the "if, then" statements act differently than normal. The "if then" statements are either entirely true or entirely false.

Assume that:

If "a" is true, then "b" is true.

If "b" is true, then "a" is true.

If "a" is false, then "b" is false.

If "b" is false, then "a" is false.

For example:

"If Ebony is sponsored by Run Co., then Billy is sponsored by Run Co."

Part "a" is about Ebony. Part "b" is about Billy. Both parts are either true or false. If you look at the grid, it becomes clear that this statement is false. Run Co. is only sponsoring three runners, and two of those runners are Cindy and Darcy. It is impossible for Run Co. to be sponsoring Billy and Ebony.

Remember, with these logic puzzles, the statements are completely true or false. In other words, Billy and Ebony must not be sponsored by Run Co. They are sponsored by Dash Co. That leaves Andy as the final person sponsored by Run Co.

		Time to Complete Race					Sponsor (fake companies)				
		5 Minutes	10 Minutes	15 Minutes	20 Minutes	25 Minutes	Dash Co.	Dash Co.	Run Co.	Run Co.	Run Co.
Runner Name	Andy			n			n	n	y	y	y
	Billy			n			y	y	n	n	n
	Cindy			n	n		n	n	y	y	y
	Darcy	n	n	y	n	n	n	n	y	y	y
	Ebony	n		n	n		y	y	n	n	n
Sponsor (fake companies)	Dash Co.			n		y					
	Dash Co.			n		y					
	Run Co.			y		n					
	Run Co.			y		n					
	Run Co.			y		n					

Listing or considering statements. These are clues that list everything in a category once, and the listed items do not relate to each other. The listed items are not in any particular order.

For example:

"The five runners are Andy, Billy, Darcy, the person who finished at 5 minutes, and the person who finished at 25 minutes."

"Runner" is the category. There are five runners, so there are five parts to the list. Each clue tells us about a different runner. From the information given, we are able to figure out that Cindy and Ebony finished at 5 or 25 minutes. Looking at the grid, we see that Ebony could only have finished at 10 or 25 minutes, so Ebony must have finished at 25 minutes. Follow the Ebony row across and put a "y" in the 25-minute box. We also know that Cindy must have finished the race in 5 minutes, so follow the Cindy row across and mark a "y" in the 5-minute box.

Make sure to put "n" in all the correct boxes.
Also, we see that Cindy is sponsored by Run Co. Make sure to mark the boxes for the 5-minute finish time for Run Co.

		Time to Complete Race					Sponsor (fake companies)				
		5 Minutes	10 Minutes	15 Minutes	20 Minutes	25 Minutes	Dash Co.	Dash Co.	Run Co.	Run Co.	Run Co.
Runner Name	Andy	n		n		n	n	n	y	y	y
	Billy	n		n		n	y	y	n	n	n
	Cindy	y	n	n	n	n	n	n	y	y	y
	Darcy	n	n	y	n	n	n	n	y	y	y
	Ebony	n	n	n	n	y	y	y	n	n	n
Sponsor (fake companies)	Dash Co.	n		n		y					
	Dash Co.	n		n		y					
	Run Co.	y		y		n					
	Run Co.	y		y		n					
	Run Co.	y		y		n					

Addition or subtraction clues. There clues involve adding or subtracting to get information.
For example:
"The time that Cindy finished plus the time Andy finished equals the time Darcy finished."

We know that Cindy finished at 5 minutes, and we know that Darcy finished at 15 minutes. We don't know when Andy finished. (5) Cindy + (?) Andy = (15) Darcy.
Let's try subtracting. $15 - 5 = 10$. Andy finished at 10 minutes.

Oh, look. Billy is the only runner left and 20 minutes is the only time left. Billy must have finished the race at 20 minutes.

You can also match up the rest of the times with the sponsors.

		Time to Complete Race					Sponsor (fake companies)				
		5 Minutes	10 Minutes	15 Minutes	20 Minutes	25 Minutes	Dash Co.	Dash Co.	Run Co.	Run Co.	Run Co.
Runner Name	Andy	n	y	n	n	n	n	n	y	y	y
	Billy	n	n	n	y	n	y	y	n	n	n
	Cindy	y	n	n	n	n	n	n	y	y	y
	Darcy	n	n	y	n	n	n	n	y	y	y
	Ebony	n	n	n	n	y	y	y	n	n	n
Sponsor (fake companies)	Dash Co.	n	n	n	y	y					
	Dash Co.	n	n	n	y	y					
	Run Co.	y	y	y	n	n					
	Run Co.	y	y	y	n	n					
	Run Co.	y	y	y	n	n					

Also, check your results with the answer key at the end of the book. The answers will be in a chart like this:

The Race		
Andy	10 Minutes	Run Co.
Billy	20 Minutes	Dash Co.
Cindy	5 Minutes	Run Co.
Darcy	15 Minutes	Run Co.
Ebony	25 Minutes	Dash Co.

Congratulations! You completed your first puzzle, but there are still some things you need to know about:

Before and after clues. These clues are based on time or numbers.
For example:
"Darcy finished the race before Billy but after Andy."
"Billy finished sometime after the runner who finished at 10 minutes."

Categories that appear multiple times. Notice how the different run times (5, 10, 15, 20, and 25 minutes) only match up with one person in the puzzle. That is how most puzzles are.
Rarely, there are categories that will match up more than once in a puzzle. In this case, it was the sponsors; who covered two and three people instead of just one.

Categories that appear multiple times in a puzzle are trickery than categories that only appear once.

For example:
When it was discovered that Darcy finished at 15 minutes, nobody else could finish at 15 minutes. "N" was put in the boxes for the other runners and 15 minutes. The same was not true when it was discovered that Cindy was sponsored by Run Co. Run Co. sponsored three racers, so after Cindy, there were still two other runners to match with Run Co.

That's it for the tutorial. Enjoy the logic puzzles.

Contents

Engagement and Wedding Plans

Recommended verses: see appendix
Difficulty: hard

Marriage is a wonderful gift from God. The following Christian couples got engaged and married over the past few months. Match the brides with their grooms, the place of proposal, the month of the wedding, and the color of the bride's dress.

Categories

Bride: Amber, Becky, Emma, Gina, Jamie, Lauren, Natalie, and Shana
Groom: Blake, Hunter, James, Jesse, Kyle, Robert, Tim, and TJ
Place of the proposal: beach, boat, bowling alley, church, fancy restaurant, park, street with a flash mob, and a waterfall
Month of the wedding: January, February, March, April, May, June, July, and August
Color of the bride's dress: blue, green, pink, red, silver, violet, white, and yellow

Clues

1. Becky married Robert or Tim, the proposal occurred in a fancy restaurant or a bowling alley, the wedding happened in July or August, and her dress was not blue or yellow.
2. Gina and Natalie were not proposed to at the beach.
3. Blake proposed to his bride in the street with a flash mob, but he did not propose to Gina.
4. Tim proposed at a church and the wedding was in August.
5. The July bride did not wear blue, red, or white.
6. TJ proposed on a boat to Amber, Emma, or Shana and got married two months before Tim.
7. Natalie married three months before the bride with the pink wedding dress and two months after Emma.
8. Blake married before Shana, who married in June.
9. Hunter, who did not marry Amber or Lauren, loved his bride's red dress in March or April.
10. Consider brides Amber, Becky, and Gina: one wore a blue dress, one wore a pink dress, and one was proposed to at a waterfall.
11. James got married in January, Emma got married in February, March's bride wore a violet dress, the proposal at a fancy restaurant led to a wedding in April, the proposal at the beach led to a wedding in May, June's bride wore a green dress, and the bride in August wore yellow.
12. Natalie married before Jamie and Lauren, but after the bride who was proposed to at the park.
13. The park proposal did not lead to a wedding in February.
14. The bride in May wore silver and she was not Emma.
15. Jesse loved seeing his bride in violet, but she was not Gina or Lauren.
16. Gina married before Amber and Lauren married before Jamie.

Grid for Engagement and Wedding Plans

	Amber	Becky	Emma	Gina	Jamie	Lauren	Natalie	Shana	Blue	Green	Pink	Red	Silver	Violet	White	Yellow	January	February	March	April	May	June	July	August	Beach	Boat	Bowling Alley	Church	Fancy Resturant	Park	Street with a Flash Mob	Waterfall
Blake																																
Hunter																																
James																																
Jesse																																
Kyle																																
Robert																																
Tim																																
TJ																																
Beach																																
Boat																																
Bowling Alley																																
Church																																
Fancy Resturant																																
Park																																
Street with a Flash Mob																																
Waterfall																																
January																																
February																																
March																																
April																																
May																																
June																																
July																																
August																																
Blue																																
Green																																
Pink																																
Red																																
Silver																																
Violet																																
White																																
Yellow																																

Choosing an Old Testament Story

Recommended verses: see appendix
Difficulty: easy

You are the kindergarten Sunday school teacher. You have asked the children to pick the story for next week's lesson. The children got to nominate their favorite stories from the Old Testament and the class voted to decide the winner. Match the child with the Old Testament story he or she suggested and the number of votes the story got.

A little bit about these stories:
1. **David and Goliath.** David, an Israelite shepherd boy, fights Goliath, a giant Philistine warrior.
2. **Elijah the Prophet.** Elijah, an Israelite prophet, goes up against King Ahab, Queen Jezebel, and their worship of the false god Baal.
3. **Noah's Ark.** A flood is coming, so Noah must quickly build an ark to keep his family and two of every animal safe.
4. **The Plagues of Egypt.** Pharaoh, the king of Egypt, will not let Moses and the Israelite slaves worship God on the mountain, so God sends plagues into Egypt.
5. **Queen Esther.** The king's trusted advisor, Haman, sends an edict to have all Jews killed in a single day. God uses Esther and Mordecai to save the day.

Categories

Student: Abby, Ben, Cadena, Darla, and Ernest
Old Testament story: "David and Goliath," "Elijah the Prophet," "Noah's Ark," "The Plagues of Egypt," and "Queen Esther"
Votes: 2, 4, 6, 8, and 10

Clues

1. "Noah's Ark" had 4 votes.
2. The story Ernest suggested had 8 or 10 votes.
3. Darla's story had more votes than Ben's, but fewer votes than Abby's.
4. Abby suggested "Elijah the Prophet" or "Queen Esther."
5. "David and Goliath" had 10 votes.
6. "Queen Esther" had two votes more than "Elijah the Prophet."
7. Ben suggested "David and Goliath" or "The Plagues of Egypt."
8. Cadena's story had 6 votes.
9. Ernest's story had more votes than "Queen Esther."

Grid for Choosing an Old Testament Story

	David and Goliath	Elijah the Prophet	Noah's Ark	The Plagues of Egypt	Queen Esther	2	4	6	8	10
Abby										
Ben										
Caden										
Darla										
Ernest										
2										
4										
6										
8										
10										

Choosing a Story about Jesus

Recommended verses: see appendix
Difficulty: easy

You are the first grade Sunday school teacher. You have announced to the class that they will start learning about Jesus. The children are very excited. Almost everyone knows a story about Jesus that he or she wants to talk about. Unfortunately, nobody is listening. You tell the class that you will choose the story about Jesus this week and that they can choose the story for next week by voting. Match the child with story he or she suggested and the number of votes the story got.

A bit about these stories:

1. **Jesus's Birth:** Shepherds and wise men are present at the birth of God's Son.
2. **Jesus Brings Lazarus Back to Life:** Lazarus dies, and Jesus brings him back to life three days later.
3. **Jesus's Death:** Jesus is tried for being the Son of God and is crucified.
4. **Jesus Feeds Five Thousand:** Jesus makes five loaves of bread and two fish lunch for five thousand men plus an unknown number of women and children.
5. **Jesus Heals a Paralyzed Man:** A paralyzed man is lowered through the roof to be healed by Jesus.
6. **Jesus Heals a Man with Demons:** A demon-possessed man terrorizes a graveyard until Jesus sends the demons into a group of pigs.
7. **Jesus's Parable of the Good Samaritan:** Jesus tells the story of man nearly beaten to death on the road.
8. **Jesus's Resurrection:** Jesus returns from the dead three days after dying.

Categories

Student: Clarissa, Harry, Logan, Rose, Simon, Willow, Yazmin, and Zola
Story about Jesus: "Jesus's Birth," "Jesus Brings Lazarus Back to Life," "Jesus's Death," "Jesus Feeds Five Thousand," "Jesus Heals a Paralyzed Man," "Jesus Heals a Man with Demons," "Jesus's Parable of the Good Samaritan," and "Jesus's Resurrection"
Votes: 1, 2, 3, 4, 5, 6, 7, and 8

Clues

1. Harry did not suggest "Jesus's Birth" or "Jesus's Parable of the Good Samaritan."
2. The story of "Jesus's Birth" got 6 votes and "Jesus's Resurrection" got 4 votes.
3. Yazmin's story was not "Jesus Heals a Man with Demons."
4. Logan's story got 6 or more votes and it was not "Jesus's Parable of the Good Samaritan."
5. Zola's story only got 3 votes, but Harry's and Willow's stories got fewer votes than that.
6. The story "Jesus Brings Lazarus Back to Life" got 5 votes, and "Jesus's Parable of the Good Samaritan" got 8 votes.
7. Clarissa did not suggest "Jesus Brings Lazarus Back to Life" or "Jesus Heals a Paralyzed Man."
8. Simon suggested "Jesus's Resurrection."
9. The stories suggested by Clarissa, Harry, Logan, and Simon each got an even number of votes.
10. The story "Jesus's Death" got 1 vote, and "Jesus Feeds Five Thousand" got 2 votes.
11. Rose suggested "Jesus's Birth" or the story with 7 votes.
12. "Jesus Heals a Man with Demons" had an odd number of votes and it got more votes than "Jesus Heals a Paralyzed Man."

Grid for Choosing a Story about Jesus

	Clarissa	Harry	Logan	Rose	Simon	Willow	Yazmin	Zola	1	2	3	4	5	6	7	8
Jesus' Birth																
Jesus Brings Lazarus Back to Life,																
Jesus' Death																
Jesus Feeds Five Thousand																
Jesus Heals a Paralyzed Man																
Jesus Heals a Man with Demons																
Jesus' Parable of the Good Samaritan																
Jesus' Resurrection																
1																
2																
3																
4																
5																
6																
7																
8																

Blessing of the Animals: Year 1

Recommended verses: see appendix
Difficulty: easy

It's the time for the blessing of the animals. Families have brought their pets to church to receive God's blessing through the pastor. You notice all kinds of animals around you. Match the family with their pet's name and the type of animal.

Categories

Family: Brown, Davidson, Everett, Irving, Peterson, Reed, Vander, and Whitterson
Pet's names: Don, Fred, Grace, Izzy, Lucky, Mimi, Stu, and Trixie
Animal: Siamese cat, tabby cat, St. Bernard, Yorkshire terrier, exotic fish, hamster, parrot, and rabbit

Clues

1. Lucky is the Siamese cat, the tabby cat, or the rabbit.
2. The Whittersons have a hamster, a parrot, or a Yorkshire terrier, and the name of their pet is Fred, Izzy, or Mimi.
3. The hamster is named Trixie.
4. Consider the animals named Don, Grace, and Mimi: one is a tabby cat, one is an exotic fish, and one is part of the Reed family.
5. The Vanders own a dog.
6. Lucky is part of the Irving family.
7. Izzy is not part of the Davidson family, and Don is not part of the Reed family.
8. Izzy curiously examined the Petersons' pet.
9. The two cats, Grace and Lucky, got along surprisingly well.
10. Stu is part of the Brown family, but he is not any kind of dog.
11. Fred is the name of the St. Bernard.
12. Mr. Peterson is allergic to pet hair, so the family owns an exotic fish.
13. The family that owns Izzy mentioned how she won a blue ribbon at the dog show.
14. Trixie is part of the Davidson or Vander families.
15. The Reed family owns a singing parrot.

Grid for Blessing of the Animals: Year 1

	Don	Fred	Grace	Izzy	Lucky	Mimi	Stu	Trixie	Cat-Siamese	Cat-Tabby	Dog- St. Bernard	Dog-Yorkshire Terrier	Exotic Fish	Hamster	Parrot	Rabbit
Brown																
Davidson																
Everett																
Irving																
Peterson																
Reed																
Vander																
Whitterson																
Cat-Siamese																
Cat-Tabby																
Dog- St. Bernard																
Dog-Yorkshire Terrier																
Exotic Fish																
Hamster																
Parrot																
Rabbit																

Blessing of the Animals: Year 2

Recommended verses: see appendix
Difficulty: medium

Once again, the blessing of the animals has arrived. Families excitedly bring their pets to church so that they can be blessed. This year, you notice a few new animals and families. Match the family with their pet's name and the type of animal.

Categories

Family: Angelou, Crawford, Eissler, Hanaway, Lyon, Mathus, Smith, Washington, and West
Pet's name: Astrid, Boomerang, Cameron, Chloe, Electra, Junnifer, Homer, Poe, and Zinnia
Animal: cockatoo, lovebird, Bengal tiger, Ragdoll cat, American Staffordshire terrier, Great Dane, Pomeranian, fancy rat, and frog

Clues

1. Cameron and Junnifer are the same kind of animal (bird, cat, or dog).
2. The Ragdoll cat belongs to the Mathus or West family.
3. The fancy rat belongs to the Eisslers or Hanaways.
4. The American Staffordshire terrier belongs to the Washington family.
5. Electra is the name of the American Staffordshire terrier or the Bengal cat or the cockatoo.
6. Homer is owned by the West family, but Homer is not a cat.
7. The Eisslers own a dog, but the dog is not named Chloe or Cameron.
8. The Angelou family owns a Great Dane, and the Smith family owns Zinnia.
9. The fancy rat is not named Astrid or Boomerang.
10. The frog is not owned by the Crawford or the Lyon family.
11. Poe was chased by the Crawford family's cat, and the Crawford family's cat was chased by Boomerang.
12. Poe did not get along Zinnia, even though they are both birds.
13. The families are as follows: one is the Angelou family, one is the Lyon family, one owns the Bengal cat, one owns a frog, one owns a lovebird, one owns a Pomeranian, one owns Astrid, one owns Chloe, and one owns Junnifer.

Grid for Blessing of the Animals: Year 2

	Angelou	Crawford	Eissler	Hanaway	Lyon	Mathus	Smith	Washington	West	Bird-Cockatoo	Bird-Lovebird	Cat-Bengal	Cat-Ragdoll	Dog-American Staffordshire	Terrier	Dog-Great Dane	Dog-Pomerian	Fancy Rat	Frog
Astrid																			
Boomerang																			
Cameron																			
Chloe																			
Electra																			
Homer																			
Junnifer																			
Poe																			
Zinnia																			
Bird-Cockatoo																			
Bird-Lovebird																			
Cat-Bengal																			
Cat-Ragdoll																			
Dog-American Staffordshire																			
Terrier																			
Dog-Great Dane																			
Dog-Pomerian																			
Fancy Rat																			
Frog																			

Blessing of the Animals: Year 3

Recommended verses: See appendix
Difficulty: medium

This is the third blessing of the animals that you have attended. As usual, many pets are here to be blessed, and everybody seems very excited. Some of the pets this year are a bit more interesting. Match the family with their pet's name and the type of animal.

Categories

Family: Brooks, Davis, Hale, Ivory, Lockhart, Moore, Noble, Pickens, and Urban
Pet's name: Digger, Fox, Lightning, Macaroni, Ruby, Slinky, Thursday, Vespera, and Yuri
Animal: sphynx cat, Persian cat, Border Collie, Labrador retriever, Staffordshire bull terrier, ferret, horse, koi fish, and snake

Clues

1. If the Lockharts own Slinky, then the Pickenses own Ruby.
2. If the Moores own Thursday, then the Ivories own Fox.
3. If Vespera is the snake, then the Hales own Digger.
4. If Lightning is owned by the Davis family, then Slinky is the ferret.
5. If the Urban family owns Macaroni, then Thursday must be the Persian cat.
6. Digger does not belong to the Brooks family, Fox does not belong to Pickenses, Thursday does not belong to the Davis family, and Yuri does not belong to the Nobles.
7. The Davis and Hale families do not own cats or dogs.
8. Digger is the ferret and he does not belong to the Lockhart family.
9. Lightning is not the ferret and Thursday is not the Staffordshire bull terrier.
10. The following are true about the Ivory, Noble, and Urban families: Fox, Macaroni, and Yuri are their pets' names. The animals are the koi fish, the Labrador retriever, and the Staffordshire bull terrier.
11. Slinky is a sphynx cat.
12. The Brooks family does not own Lightning or the border collie.
13. The Moore family does not own the horse named Ruby, but they do own Thursday.
14. Consider the Brooks, Lockhart, and Pickens families: one owns the sphynx cat, one owns a horse, and one owns Lightning.
15. Fox is not a dog, Vespera is not a cat, Macaroni is not the Labrador retriever, and the sphynx cat is not owned by the Lockharts.
16. The Pickens family owns Lightning.

Grid for Blessing of the Animals: Year 3

	Brooks	Davis	Hale	Ivory	Lockhart	Moore	Noble	Pickens	Urban	Cat-Sphynx	Cat-Persian	Dog-Border Collie	Dog-Labrador Retriever	Dog-Staffordshire Bull Terrier	Ferret	Horse	Koi Fish	Snake
Digger																		
Fox																		
Lightening																		
Macaroni																		
Ruby																		
Slinky																		
Thursday																		
Vespera																		
Yuri																		
Cat-Sphynx																		
Cat-Persian																		
Dog-Border Collie																		
Dog-Labrador Retriever																		
Dog-Staffordshire Bull Terrier																		
Ferret																		
Horse																		
Koi Fish																		
Snake																		

Youth Volunteers

Recommended verses: See appendix
Difficulty: easy

The youth have decided to grow and learn by volunteering in various service events at their churches. Volunteering gives them a greater understanding of empathy, people, and the problems that are in the world. Match the name of the youth with the event he or she is serving at and the person who recommended the event.

Categories

Youth volunteer: George, Harriet, Patrick, Megan, Natasha, and Rachel
Event: Differently-Abled Dance, English as a Second Language Class, Fundraiser to Cure Lupus, Souper Bowl, Thanksgiving Dinner for the Retirement Home, and Vacation Bible School
People who made recommendations: friend, grandparents, nobody, parent, pastor, and teacher

Clues

1. The Thanksgiving Dinner for the Retirement Home was recommended by nobody or the pastor.
2. The Fundraiser to Cure Lupus was recommended by a friend or grandparents.
3. Rachel volunteered for the Differently-Abled Dance or the English as a Second Language class.
4. Patrick volunteered for the English as a Second Language class or Vacation Bible School.
5. Harriet participated in the Fundraiser to Cure Lupus or the Souper Bowl
6. The recommendation for the Souper Bowl came from a parent.
7. The recommendation George got was from a friend.
8. The recommendation Rachel got was from the pastor.
9. Consider Megan and Natasha: one volunteered at the Fundraiser to Cure Lupus and the other volunteered at the Thanksgiving Dinner for the Retirement Home.
10. Natasha got her recommendation from nobody or a teacher.
11. Patrick and Rachel have one of the following statements true about each of them: one volunteered for the English as a Second Language class and one got a recommendation from a teacher.

Grid for Youth Volunteers

	George	Harriet	Megan	Patrick	Natasha	Rachel	Friend	Parent	Grandparent	Teacher	Nobody	Pastor
Differently-Abled Dance												
English as a Second												
Language Class												
Fundraiser to cure Lupus												
Soup'er Bowl												
Thanksgiving Dinner for the Retirement Home												
Vacation Bible School												
Friend												
Grandparent												
Nobody												
Parent												
Pastor												
Teacher												

Global Mission Trips

Recommended verses: See appendix
Difficulty: hard

Several churches are sending members on mission trips across the globe to proclaim the Word of God, to show God's love, and to serve the local residents. Match the name of the church with the location and the duration of the trip.

Please note that the names of the following churches are purely fictional.

Categories

Name of church: Blessed Be, Christ the King, Cross and Crown, Holy Trinity, Resurrection, Redeemer, St. Mark's, St. Mary's, and St. Peter's
Location: Cuba, Haiti, India, Japan, Kuwait, Mexico, South Africa, Russia, and United States
Duration of trip: 2 weeks, 3 weeks, 4 weeks, 5 weeks, 6 weeks, 7 weeks, 8 weeks, 9 weeks, and 10 weeks

Clues

1. Blessed Be is not going to Haiti, Christ the King is not going to Mexico, Cross and Crown is not going to Cuba, and Holy Trinity is not going to the United States.
2. Consider the mission trips to South Africa and Kuwait: one will be 3 weeks long and the other will be 7 weeks long.
3. The mission trip to India will be four weeks longer than the mission trip done by Blessed Be.
4. Christ the King will be gone for 2 weeks, but not to Cuba, Haiti, or the United States.
5. The different mission trips are as follows: one will be done by Redeemer, one will be done by Resurrection, one will be done by St. Mary's, one is going to Russia, one is going to South Africa, one is going to the United States, one will last 4 weeks, one will last 7 weeks, and one will last 8 weeks.
6. The mission trip to Japan is longer than the mission trip to Russia, but the mission trip to Japan is three weeks shorter than the mission trip done by Cross and Crown.
7. If St. Mark's is going to Mexico, then Blessed Be is going to Cuba.
8. If St. Mark's is not going to Mexico, then St. Mary's is going to Mexico.
9. The mission trip done by Redeemer will last more than 6 weeks.
10. The mission trip done by St. Peter's will not be 3, 5, or 10 weeks long, and St. Peter's is not going to Japan or Mexico.
11. The trip to Cuba will last for 9 weeks and will be done by Redeemer or Resurrection.
12. Consider the mission trips to India, Mexico, and the United States: one will be done by St. Peter's, one will last 5 weeks, and one will last 10 weeks.
13. The trip to South Africa is exactly half the length of the trip taken by Resurrection.
14. The trip by St. Mark's will be shorter than the trip by St. Mary's.

Grid for Global Mission Trips

	Blessed Be	Christ the King	Cross and Crown	Holy Trinity	Redeemer	Resurrection	St. Mark's	St. Mary's	St. Peter's	2 Weeks	3 Weeks	4 Weeks	5 Weeks	6 Weeks	7 Weeks	8 Weeks	9 Weeks	10 Weeks
Cuba																		
Haiti																		
India																		
Japan																		
Kuwait																		
Mexico																		
Russia																		
South Africa																		
United States																		
2 Weeks																		
3 Weeks																		
4 Weeks																		
5 Weeks																		
6 Weeks																		
7 Weeks																		
8 Weeks																		
9 Weeks																		
10 Weeks																		

Mission Trips in Africa

Recommended verses: See appendix
Difficulty: medium

Several churches are sending members on mission trips throughout Africa to proclaim the Word of God, to show God's love, and to serve the local residents. Match the name of the church with the location and the duration of the trip.

Please note that the names of the following churches are purely fictional.

Categories

Name of church: All Are Welcome, Community of Believers, International, Led by Faith, Many Blessings, Pine Valley, and Solid Rock
Location: Angola, Botswana, Egypt, Gambia, Morocco, Sudan, and Zimbabwe
Duration of trip: 3 weeks, 4 weeks, 5 weeks, 6 weeks, 7 weeks, 8 weeks, and 9 weeks

Clues

1. The churches that are going on a mission trip for an odd number of weeks are All Are Welcome, Led by Faith, Many Blessings, and Solid Rock.
2. The places that are visited for an even number of weeks are Angola, Botswana, and Morocco.
3. If All Are Welcome is going to Morocco, then Led by Faith is going to Sudan.
4. If Community of Believers is going to Egypt, then Pine Valley is going to Botswana.
5. If International is going to Angola, then Many Blessings will be gone 5 weeks or less.
6. If Led by Faith is going on a trip for 7 weeks, then Solid Rock is going on a trip for 3 weeks.
7. If the trip to Botswana is 4 weeks, then the trip to Morocco is 5 weeks.
8. The 9-week trip will be with All Are Welcome, and the trip will not be to Egypt.
9. The 3-week trip will be to Sudan or Zimbabwe, and it will not be done by Solid Rock.
10. Many Blessings is going to Egypt.
11. Community of Believers will be gone more than 5 weeks, but fewer weeks than the trip to Morocco.
12. The mission trips are as follows: one is with All Are Welcome, one is International, one is going to Botswana, one is going to Egypt, one is going for 3 weeks, one is going for 4 weeks, and one is going for 5 weeks.
13. The trip to Gambia is longer than the trip to Sudan.

Grid for Mission Trips in Africa

	All Are Welcome	Community of Believers	International	Led by Faith	Many Blessings	Pine Valley	Solid Rock	3 weeks	4 weeks	5 weeks	6 weeks	7 weeks	8 weeks	9 weeks
Angola														
Botswana														
Egypt														
Gambia														
Morocco														
Sudan														
Zimbabwe														
3 weeks														
4 weeks														
5 weeks														
6 weeks														
7 weeks														
8 weeks														
9 weeks														

Mission Trips in Asia

Recommended verses: See appendix
Difficulty: medium

Several churches are sending members on mission trips throughout Africa to proclaim the Word of God, to show God's love, and to serve the local residents. Match the name of the church with the location and the duration of the trip.

Please note that the names of the following churches are purely fictional.

Categories

Name of church: Blessed Mary, City of Faith, Hill Top, Living Shepherd, Mt. of Olives, New Hope, Serenity, United

Location: China, Iran, Myanmar, North Korea, Saudi Arabia, Thailand, Vietnam, and Yemen

Duration of trip: 2 weeks, 3 weeks, 4 weeks, 5 weeks, 6 weeks, 7 weeks, 8 weeks, and 9 weeks

Clues

1. The trip done by New Hope will be three weeks longer than the trip to Thailand, but two weeks shorter than the trip by Mt. of Olives.
2. Blessed Mary is going to China, Saudi Arabia, or Vietnam, and they will be gone for more than 6 weeks.
3. If Hill Top is going to Saudi Arabia, then United is going to Thailand.
4. If Hill Top is going for 9 weeks, then Living Shepherd is leaving for 7 weeks.
5. If Hill Top is going for 5 weeks, then City of Faith is going to Vietnam.
6. Living Shepherd, Mt. of Olives, and New Hope will be gone for 5, 7, and 9 weeks, and they will not be going to China or Saudi Arabia.
7. The Myanmar and Vietnam mission trips will be fewer than 7 weeks long.
8. The mission trips are as follows: City of Faith will be gone for 2 weeks, New Hope will be gone for 7 weeks, United will be gone for 4 weeks, the trip to China will last 8 weeks, the trip to Iran will last 5 weeks, the trip to Saudi Arabia will last 3 weeks, the trip to Vietnam will last 6 weeks, and the trip to Yemen will last 9 weeks.
9. Serenity is not going to Saudi Arabia.

Grid for Mission Trips in Asia

	Blessed Mary	City of Faith	Hill Top	Living Shepherd	Mt. of Olives	New Hope	Serenity	United	2 Weeks	3 Weeks	4 Weeks	5 Weeks	6 Weeks	7 Weeks	8 Weeks	9 Weeks
China																
Iran																
Myanmar																
North Korea																
Saudi Arabia																
Thailand																
Vietnam																
Yemen																
2 Weeks																
3 Weeks																
4 Weeks																
5 Weeks																
6 Weeks																
7 Weeks																
8 Weeks																
9 Weeks																

Mission Trips in Europe

Recommended verses: See appendix
Difficulty: medium

Several churches are sending members on mission trips throughout South America to proclaim the Word of God, to show God's love, and to serve the local residents. Match the name of the church with the location and the duration of the trip.

Please note that the names of the following churches are purely fictional.

Categories

Name of church: Bethany, Community of the Cross, Discipleship, Grace, Mt. Hope, Peace, Southside, and Woodland

Location: France, Germany, Iceland, Italy, Spain, Sweden, Romania, and the United Kingdom

Duration of trip: 2 weeks, 3 weeks, 4 weeks, 5 weeks, 6 weeks, 7 weeks, 8 weeks, and 9 weeks

Clues

1. If Bethany is going to Italy, then the trip to Romania will be 7 weeks long.
2. If Bethany is going to Spain, then the trip to Germany will be 6 weeks long.
3. If Community of the Cross is going to Sweden, then Peace is going to France.
4. If Community of the Cross is going to the United Kingdom, then Mt. Hope is going to Romania.
5. If Discipleship will be on a trip for 2 weeks, then the trip to France will be 3 weeks.
6. If Discipleship will be on a trip for 4 weeks, then the trip to Germany will be 7 weeks.
7. If Mt. Hope is going on a trip for 5 weeks or less, then the trip to Italy will be 2 weeks, the trip to the United Kingdom will be 3 weeks, and the trip to France will be 4 weeks.
8. If Mt. Hope is going on a trip for 6 or more weeks, then the trip to Germany will be 3 weeks, and the trip to the United Kingdom will be 7 or 8 weeks.
9. If Southside is not going to Italy, then the trip to Spain will not be 5, 6, or 7 weeks.
10. If Southside is going to Italy, then the trip to France will be 5 weeks, the trip to Sweden will be 6 weeks, and the trip to Spain will be 7 weeks.
11. If Woodland is going to Spain, then the trip to Spain will last 4 weeks.
12. If Woodland is going to France, then the trip to France will last 7 weeks.
13. If Woodland is going to Romania, the trip to Romania will last 7 weeks.
14. Discipleship's trip will be 6 weeks, Mt. Hope's trip will be 8 weeks, Southside's trip will be 5 weeks, and the trip to Iceland will be 9 weeks.
15. Grace is going to Iceland, Peace is going to Spain, and Woodland is going to Romania.

Grid for Mission Trips in Europe

	Bethany	Community of the Cross	Discipleship	Grace	Mt. Hope	Peace	Southside	Woodland	2 Weeks	3 Weeks	4 Weeks	5 Weeks	6 Weeks	7 Weeks	8 Weeks	9 Weeks
France																
Germany																
Iceland																
Italy																
Spain																
Sweden																
Romania																
United Kingdom																
2 Weeks																
3 Weeks																
4 Weeks																
5 Weeks																
6 Weeks																
7 Weeks																
8 Weeks																
9 Weeks																

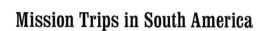

Mission Trips in South America

Recommended verses: See appendix
Difficulty: easy

Several churches are sending members on mission trips throughout South America to proclaim the Word of God, to show God's love, and to serve the local residents. Match the name of the church with the location and the duration of the trip.

Please note that the names of the following churches are purely fictional.

Categories

Name of church: Celestial, Freedom, Heavenly Father, New Life, Oasis, Pilgrim, St. Matthew, and Zion
Location: Argentina, Brazil, Chile, Ecuador, Peru, Suriname, Uruguay, and Venezuela
Duration of trip: 2 weeks, 3 weeks, 4 weeks, 5 weeks, 6 weeks, 7 weeks, 8 weeks, and 9 weeks

Clues

1. Celestial is going to Chile or Suriname or Uruguay, and Oasis is going to Brazil or Peru.
2. Consider the trips to Ecuador, Peru, and Uruguay: one will be with Heavenly Father, one will be with St. Matthew, and one will be 7 weeks long.
3. The trip done by Freedom will be two weeks longer than the trip to Peru.
4. The trip to Argentina will be 6 weeks, and it will be done by Heavenly Father or Zion.
5. Celestial will be gone two weeks more than Zion.
6. The trip to Chile will last fewer than 5 weeks, but the trip to Brazil and the trip done by Freedom will last more than 5 weeks.
7. New Life's trip and the trip to Uruguay will last an even number of weeks.
8. Freedom is going to Ecuador for fewer than 8 weeks.
9. The trip to Venezuela will be 2 or 3 weeks.
10. New Life is not going to Venezuela, and Oasis is not going to Peru.
11. Heavenly Father will be gone for 2 weeks.

Grid for Mission Trip in South America

	Celestial	Freedom	Heavenly Father	New Life	Oasis	Pilgrim	St. Matthew	Zion	2 Weeks	3 Weeks	4 Weeks	5 Weeks	6 Weeks	7 Weeks	8 Weeks	9 Weeks
Argentina																
Brazil																
Chile																
Ecuador																
Peru																
Suriname																
Uruguay																
Venezuela																
2 Weeks																
3 Weeks																
4 Weeks																
5 Weeks																
6 Weeks																
7 Weeks																
8 Weeks																
9 Weeks																

Mission Trips in the United States

Recommended verses: See appendix
Difficulty: easy

Several churches are sending members on mission trips throughout the United States to proclaim the Word of God, to show God's love, and to serve the local residents. Match the name of the church with the location and the duration of the trip.

Please note that the names of the following churches are purely fictional.

Categories

Name of church: All Nations, Church of God, First, Living Water, My Redeemer Lives, New Jerusalem, St. Luke's, and Way, Truth, and Life
Location: California, Kansas, Louisiana, Michigan, New York, Oregon, South Carolina, and Texas
Duration of trip: 2 weeks, 3 weeks, 4 weeks, 5 weeks, 6 weeks, 7 weeks, 8 weeks, and 9 weeks

Clues

1. The different mission trips are as follows: one is going to Louisiana, one is going to South Carolina, one is going to Texas, one will last for 3 weeks, one will last 4 weeks, one will last for 7 weeks, one will be with All Nations, and one will be with St. Luke's.
2. The mission trips to California, Kansas, and Louisiana will last 2, 6, and 7 weeks.
3. The mission trips to Michigan, New York, and Oregon will be done with the churches named All Nations, Church of God, and First.
4. The mission trips to South Carolina and Texas will be done by My Redeemer and New Jerusalem.
5. The 2-, 3-, and 4-week mission trips will be done by Church of God, First, and Way, Truth, and Life.
6. The 5-, 6-, and 7-week mission trips will occur in California, Kansas, and Michigan.
7. The 8- and 9-week mission trips will occur in Texas and South Carolina.
8. St. Luke's is not going to Kansas.
9. Church of God is not going to Oregon, but Church of God will be gone for 3 weeks.
10. The trip to South Carolina is 9 weeks, and the trip by My Redeemer lives is 8 weeks.

Grid for Mission Trips in the United States

	All Nations	Church of God	First	Living Water	My Redeemer Lives	New Jerusalem	St. Luke's	Way, Truth, and Life	2 Weeks	3 Weeks	4 Weeks	5 Weeks	6 Weeks	7 Weeks	8 Weeks	9 Weeks
California																
Kansas																
Louisiana																
Michigan																
New York																
Oregon																
South Carolina																
Texas																
2 Weeks																
3 Weeks																
4 Weeks																
5 Weeks																
6 Weeks																
7 Weeks																
8 Weeks																
9 Weeks																

Armor of God

Recommended verses: See appendix
Difficulty: easy

A group of mentors is teaching their mentees about the armor of God. Each mentor made one piece of armor to show their mentee. The art skills of each mentor vary, so each model is made differently. Match the name of the mentor with the name of the mentee, the piece of the armor of God, and the model.

The Armor of God is a spiritual suit of armor, not a physical one. Here is what each piece represents: [1]

1. **Belt of Truth:** Stands for truthfulness. It is about knowing God and struggling against the devil's lies.
2. **Breastplate of Righteousness:** Stands for God's righteousness, which protects our minds and emotions from the devil.
3. **Helmet of Salvation:** Offers protection from discouragement and doubt. It reminds us that God is victorious in the past, present, and the future.
4. **Shield of Faith:** Stands for faith given by the Holy Spirit. It deflects the anger, negativity, and temptations of the devil that are thrown the target, like arrows toward a bullseye.
5. **Shoes to Spread the Gospel of Peace:** Stands for the God's protection of believers and the peace believers feel.
6. **Sword of the Spirit:** Stands for the Word of God. It attacks the devil head-on and breaks his hold on people.

Categories

Name of mentor: April, Diamond, Jabari, Lavinia, Tony, and William
Name of mentee: Blaine, Calvin, Elizabeth, Gus, Isabelle, and Pauline
Piece of armor: Belt of Truth, Breastplate of Righteousness, Helmet of Salvation, Shield of Faith, Shoes to Spread the Gospel of Peace, and the Sword of the Spirit
Model: aluminum foil figure, colored-pencil sketch, magazine collage, metal figure, painting, and wooden figure

Clues

1. The mentors are as follows: one was Gus's, one was Isabelle's, one created the magazine collage, one created the painting, one created the Shield of Faith, and one created the Sword of the Spirit.
2. Jabari, Tony, and William are paired with Blaine, Calvin, and Gus.
3. Consider Elizabeth and Isabelle: one of their mentors created the Belt of Truth, and one created the Shoes to Spread the Gospel of Peace.
4. The magazine collage was not of the Belt of Truth or the Helmet of Salvation.
5. Calvin's mentor did not make the metal figure, but his mentor did make the Shield of Faith.
6. Lavinia created the painting or the wooden figure.
7. Jabari created the colored-pencil sketch or the magazine collage.
8. Blaine's mentor created the Breastplate of Righteousness.
9. Pauline's mentor created the wooden figure.
10. The Helmet of Salvation was the metal figure.
11. April made the Sword of the Spirit.
12. William made the Breastplate of Righteousness.
13. Diamond created the Belt of Truth.

---

[1] MacArthur, John. "The Believer's Armor: God's Provision for Your Protection." Grace To You. Accessed July 26, 2016.

Grid for Armor of God

	April	Diamond	Jabari	Lavinia	Tony	William	Aluminum Foil Figure	Colored-Pencil Sketch	Magazine Collage	Metal Figure	Painting	Wooden Figure	Belt of Truth	Brest Plate of Righteousness	Helmet of Salvation	Shield of Faith	Shoes to Spread the	Gospel of Peace	Sword of the Spirit
Blaine																			
Calvin																			
Elizabeth																			
Gus																			
Isabelle																			
Pauline																			
Belt of Truth																			
Brest Plate of Righteousness																			
Helmet of Salvation																			
Shield of Faith																			
Shoes to Spread the Gospel of Peace																			
Sword of the Spirit																			
Aluminum Foil Figure																			
Colored-Pencil Sketch																			
Magazine Collage																			
Metal Figure																			
Painting																			
Wooden Figure																			

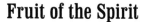

Fruit of the Spirit

Recommended verses: See appendix
Difficulty: hard

A local Bible study recently ended a series on the Fruit of the Spirit. Each week, a different person gave a presentation about a different Fruit of the Spirit. Also, the person presenting brought in a piece of fruit as a prop. Match the week of the presentation with the Fruit of the Spirit, the person presenting, and the fruit prop.

These are the Fruits of the Spirit:[2]
1. **Faithfulness.** It is being dependable, loyal, and trustworthy.
2. **Forbearance.** Also known as patience, it is thinking before you speak and being slow to anger.
3. **Gentleness.** It is being humble, calm, and nonthreatening.
4. **Goodness.** It is being generous and open-hearted.
5. **Joy.** It is unconditional happiness.
6. **Kindness.** It is gentleness, mercy, and sweetness.
7. **Love.** It seeks the best for others.
8. **Peace.** It is unity between people.
9. **Self-Control.** It is managing your behavior.

Categories

Week: week 1, week 2, week 3, week 4, week 5, week 6, week 7, and week 8
Name: Elle, Fritz, Gwen, Heidi, Ivan, Marley, Orson, Russell, and Zeke
Fruit of the Spirit: faithfulness, forbearance, gentleness, goodness, joy, kindness, love, peace, and self-control
Fruit prop: bananas, blueberries, cherries, grapes, lemon, oranges, pears, pineapples, and watermelon

Clues

1. Weeks 1, 2, and 3 only had one of the following true about each of them: one had Ivan as the presenter, one had cherries as a prop, and one had the lesson about joy.
2. Heidi presented on kindness, but not on an odd-numbered week and not with watermelon.
3. Elle presented on peace or self-control, and the prop she used was blueberries, lemons, or pears.
4. Weeks 7, 8, and 9 have presentations given by Elle, Russell, and Zeke.
5. Week 2 had pears as a prop, and week 8 had pineapples as a prop.
6. Marley used bananas as a prop, but not for faithfulness, peace, or self-control, and she presented after week 3.
7. Forbearance was presented on week 7, but the prop was not lemons, pears, or watermelon.
8. Orson used cherries as a prop, but not for self-control.
9. Consider Ivan and Russell: one was teaching about love, and one was teaching on week 2.
10. Blueberries were the prop for peace, lemons were the prop for kindness, and oranges were the prop Fritz used.
11. The themes of weeks 5 and 6 were goodness and self-control, and they were presented by Gwen and Marley.
12. If forbearance was presented by Fritz, then Marley presented on week 5.
13. If forbearance was presented by Gwen, then gentleness was presented by Ivan.
14. If Gwen presented on self-control, then the fruit prop for week 3 was oranges.

---

[2] "Fruit of the Spirit: Laminated Wall Chart." Rose Publishing, 2004. Accessed July 16, 2016.

Grid for Fruit of the Spirit

	Elle	Fritz	Gwen	Heidi	Ivan	Marley	Orson	Russell	Zeke	Bananas	Blueberries	Cherries	Grapes	Lemon	Oranges	Pears	Pineapples	Watermelon	Week 1	Week 2	Week 3	Week 4	Week 5	Week 6	Week 7	Week 8	Week 9
Faithfulness																											
Forbearance																											
Gentleness																											
Goodness																											
Joy																											
Kindness																											
Love																											
Peace																											
Self-Control																											
Week 1																											
Week 2																											
Week 3																											
Week 4																											
Week 5																											
Week 6																											
Week 7																											
Week 8																											
Week 9																											
Bananas																											
Blueberries																											
Cherries																											
Grapes																											
Lemon																											
Oranges																											
Pears																											
Pineapple																											
Watermelon																											

Teaching the Ten Commandments

Recommended verses: See appendix

Difficulty: easy

A local Bible study is focusing on the Ten Commandments. A different person will lead the lesson on a different commandment. Each person drew a random commandment from out of a hat. Match the person with the commandment he or she is teaching about.

The Ten Commandments are not a set of rules, but a rare set of gifts. Think about it:[3]

1. **No other gods:** The gift of God's self to you.
2. **No idols:** The gift of not perceiving God as limited to an image or object.
3. **Don't misuse God's name:** The gift of an intimate name that can banish demons and move mountains.
4. **Keep the Sabbath day holy:** The gift of physical rest and time spent with God.
5. **Honor parents:** The gift of parents.[4]
6. **No killing:** The gift of life and the respect of life.
7. **No adultery:** The gift of marriage and sex. Also protects you from negative consequences like STDs, unplanned pregnancies, and so on.
8. **No stealing:** The gift of property. Also puts moral responsibility on debtors and tax collectors.
9. **No false witnesses:** This is the gift of honesty and justice.
10. **No coveting:** The gift of value gratefulness.

Categories

Presenter: Avery, Franklin, Holly, Josephine, Lola, Malcolm, Odelia, Tanner, Vince, and Zahra

The Ten Commandments: no other gods, no idols, don't misuse God's name, keep the Sabbath day holy, honor parents, no killing, no adultery, no stealing, no false witnesses, and no coveting

Clues

1. Lola is not teaching about honoring parents, no killing, or no adultery.
2. Avery or Josephine is teaching about no other gods.
3. Vince or Zahra is teaching about not stealing.
4. Franklin or Odelia is teaching about not coveting.
5. Holly or Tanner is teaching about no false witnesses.
6. If Malcolm is teaching about no adultery, then Avery is teaching about keeping the Sabbath day holy.
7. If Malcolm is not teaching about no adultery, then Holly is teaching about keeping the Sabbath day holy.
8. Zahra is teaching about not killing, and Malcom is teaching about no adultery.
9. Consider Lola and Odelia: one is teaching about no coveting, and one is teaching about no idols.
10. If Tanner is teaching about no idols, then Franklin is teaching about not misusing God's name.
11. If Tanner is not teaching about no idols, then Holly is teaching about no false witnesses.

---

[3] Luker, Lamonte. "Survey of the Old Testament Class." Lutheran Theological Southern Seminary, Columbia, SC. Lecture. Fall 2014.

[4] There are several commandments that seem straightforward but are more complicated in situations like abuse, rape, accidental killing, and so on. If you have questions on the Ten Commandments, you should consult a God-fearing, well-educated pastor or clergy member and the Bible. Remember, the Ten Commandments were not meant to condemn or to cause harm. They are gifts of love.

Grid for Teaching the Ten Commandments

	Avery	Franklin	Holly	Josephine	Lola	Malcolm	Odelia	Tanner	Vince	Zahra
No Other gods										
No Idols										
Don't Misuse God's Name										
Keep the Sabbath Day Holy										
Honor Parents										
No Killing										
No Adultery										
No Stealing										
No False Witnesses										
No Coveting										

The Trinity: Father, Son, and Holy Spirit

Recommended verses: See appendix

Difficulty: easy

One of the core components of Christianity is monotheism: the belief in one God. Christians talk about God the Father, Son, and the Holy Spirit as one being. This relationship is one of the greatest mysteries of faith, yet the Trinity helps explain it. Human knowledge is not perfect, so each explanation of the Trinity is not perfect.

These four Christians are trying to explain the Trinity to their friends. They each use the first example that pops into their mind and a word that describes the Trinity. Match the name of the Christian, the example used, and the word that describes the Trinity.

Here are a few explanations of the Trinity:

1. **A finished cake:** A cake is one thing made of three or more ingredients (cake mix, water, eggs, etc.). You cannot take one of the ingredients out of the finished cake. Once the mix, water, and eggs are stirred together, there is no separating them.
2. **A three-leaf clover:** A clover has three easily distinguishable leaves, yet the three leaves still make one clover.
3. **A person:** A man can be a son, a father, and a brother at the same time, without being a contradiction. Likewise, a woman can be a daughter, a mother, and a sister at the same time.
4. **Water:** It takes the form of a solid, a liquid, and a gas, yet ice cubes, drinking water, and vapor are water nonetheless.

Categories

Name: Arianna, Coby, Michael, and Spencer

Trinity example: finished cake, three-leaf clover, person, and water

Word: essence, love, relationship, and unity

Clues

1. Arianna described the Trinity using the word "essence" or "relationship."
2. Michael explained the Trinity using the example of the finished cake or water.
3. Spencer talked about the Trinity in terms of God's love.
4. The example of the Trinity as a person was explained with the word "love" or "relationship."
5. Coby used the example of water to explain the Trinity.
6. The person who talked about the Trinity as a finished cake used the term "unity."
7. The term "essence" was used when describing the Trinity as water.
8. Spencer used a three-leaf clover.

Grid for The Trinity: Father, Son, and Holy Spirit

	Arianna	Coby	Michael	Spencer	Essence	Love	Relationship	Unity
Finished Cake								
Person								
Three-Leaved Clover								
Water								
Essence								
Love								
Relationship								
Unity								

A Pastor's Day

Recommended verses: See appendix
Difficulty: easy

Who says that pastors only work one day a week? Pastors work all week, balancing various responsibilities in the church and community as well as their own health, families, and free time. This pastor has had a very busy day. Match what this pastor did with the time he or she did it.

Categories

Time: 8 a.m., 10 a.m., 12 p.m., 2 p.m., 4 p.m., 6 p.m., and 8 p.m.
Activity: attend council meeting, meet with congregants, prayer and silent meditation, read Bible, reviewing notes for Thursday's funeral, start writing sermon, and visit sick and shut-ins

Clues

1. Meeting with congregants happens at 12 p.m. or 2 p.m.
2. Reading the Bible happens before the council meeting.
3. Reading the Bible happens after visiting the sick and shut-ins.
4. The council meeting happens after 12 p.m., but before 8 p.m.
5. Visiting the sick and shut-ins happens two hours before meeting with the congregants.
6. Prayer and meditation occurs ten hours before the council meeting.
7. Reviewing notes for Thursday's funeral happens after 4 p.m.
8. The pastor will start writing the sermon at 4 p.m.

Grid for A Pastor's Day

	8:00 AM	10:00 AM	12:00 PM	2:00 PM	4:00 PM	6:00 PM	8:00 PM
Attend Council meeting							
Meet with congregants							
Prayer and silent mediation							
Read Bible							
Reviewing notes for Thursday's funeral							
Start writing sermon							
Visit sick and shut-ins							

Christian Lecture Series

Recommended verses: See appendix
Difficulty: medium

A series of Christian lectures is being held at a building on Saturday. This is an exciting opportunity for you to learn about a subject that is important to you. You can learn what the Bible, church doctrine, and theology say about these important and sometimes controversial topics. Match the room number with the name of the professor and class.

Categories

Room Number: 101, 102, 103, 104, 105, 106, 107, 108, 109, 110, 111, and 112
Professor: Prof. Boyle, Prof. Calloway, Prof. Fjord, Prof. Green, Prof. Hill, Prof. Knowlin, Prof. Mirse, Prof. Price, Prof. Quentin, Prof. Ratcliffe, Prof. Sterling, and Prof. White
Class: Abortion, Depression and Suicide, Evangelism, Evolution, Gay and Lesbian Marriage, Marriage and Divorce, Money and Economics, Parenting, Refugees, Relationships and Sex, the Death Penalty, and Women Preachers

Clues

1. Hill, Quentin, and Ratcliffe are not in rooms 105–110.
2. Boyle, Knowlin, Price, and Sterling are not in rooms 102, 105, 108, or 109.
3. These classes are in a room with an even number: Depression and Suicide, Evolution, Gay and Lesbian Marriage, Refugees, Relationships and Sex, and the Death Penalty.
4. The Refugee class is in room 102, but the professor is not Fjord, Green, Quentin, or White.
5. The Evangelism class is in room 111, but the professor is not Boyle, Green, Price, or Ratcliffe.
6. Mirse's class is the Depression and Suicide class or the Gay and Lesbian Marriage class.
7. Consider Calloway, Fjord, and White: one teaches the Abortion class, one teaches the Parenting class, and one is in room 109.
8. Green's class is two rooms after Knowlin's class, and Sterling's class is five doors before Quentin's class.
9. The classes in rooms 107–110 are Abortion, Depression and Suicide, Evolution, and Marriage and Divorce.
10. Fjord teaches in room 101 or 103.
11. Consider Hill, Mirse, and Price: one teaches the Refugees class, one is in room 108, and one is in room 112.
12. Ratcliffe teaches the Gay and Lesbian Marriage class, and Calloway teaches Marriage and Divorce class.
13. The Death Penalty class is not taught by Hill or Sterling, and the Women Preachers class is not taught by Knowlin.

Grid for Christian Lecture Series

	101	102	103	104	105	106	107	108	109	110	111	112	Abortion	Depression & Suicide	Evangelism	Evolution	Gay & Lesbian Marriage	Marriage & Divorce	Money & Economics	Parenting	Refugees	Relationships & Sex	The Death Penalty	Women Preachers
Boyle																								
Calloway																								
Fjord																								
Green																								
Hill																								
Knowlin																								
Mirse																								
Price																								
Quentin																								
Ratcliffe																								
Sterling																								
White																								
Abortion																								
Depression & Suicide																								
Evangelism																								
Evolution																								
Gay & Lesbian Marriage																								
Marriage & Divorce																								
Money & Economics																								
Parenting																								
Refugees																								
Relationships & Sex																								
The Death Penalty																								
Women Preachers																								

Seminary Class Schedule

Recommended verses: See appendix
Difficulty: hard

When God calls you to public ministry or chaplaincy, you usually complete some kind of formal training. This training usually involves going to a seminary. Seminary is a school where you learn about your religion. Classes are challenging, the amount of homework is staggering, and most professors use complicated, theological terms in everyday conversations. Below are the names of classes, the names of professors, the day of the class, the number of books, and the advice given by upperclassmen for passing the class. Match them all, if you can.

Categories

Class: Church History, Diaconal Ministry, Ethics, Greek, Hebrew, New Testament, Old Testament, Pastoral Care, Preaching, Sacraments, Teaching, and Theology
Professor: Prof. Albom, Prof. Cena, Prof. DiCamillo, Prof. Gutiérrez, Prof. Hyland, Prof. Keller, Prof. Miller, Prof. Overett, Prof. Paris, Prof. Swinton, Prof. Thornton, and Prof. Winters
Day (three classes a day): Monday, Tuesday, Wednesday, and Thursday
Number of books (each number applies to two classes): 2, 3, 4, 5, 6, and 7

Advice (note the number):

1. Pray hard.
2. Focus on vocabulary.
3. Study two hours every day.
4. Take detailed notes.
5. Make sure the papers you write contain solid theology.
6. Never skip homework.
7. Write to be understood by scholars and congregants.
8. The professor wants you to question him or her in class.
9. Diligence is what you learn from trying, and humility is what you learn from failing the first three times.
10. Be creative.
11. Repeat exactly what the professor says.
12. Only read the required books.

Clues

1. Advice number 9 is given for the Hebrew class, which is taught by Cena, Keller, or Overett.
2. Tuesday classes are taught by DiCamillo, Miller, and Winters.
3. Advice number 5 is given about Sacraments class, advice number 11 is given about Gutiérrez's class, and advice number 12 was given to Paris's class.
4. Monday classes are Diaconal Ministry, Hebrew, and Sacraments.
5. The number of books in each class are as follows (no classes are repeated): Diaconal Ministry has 3, Greek has 4, Hebrew has 2, New Testament has 5, Old Testament has 4, Theology has 7, Albom's class has 2, Gutiérrez's class has 6, Hyland's class has 6, Keller's class has 7, Overett's class has 3, and Winters's class has 5.
6. Advice number 2, number 4, and number 8 were given to Wednesday classes.
7. Church History, New Testament, Old Testament, and Pastoral Care are not Wednesday classes.

8. Miller teaches Greek or Theology with 4 textbooks, and Thornton teaches Ethics or Theology with 7 textbooks.

9. Preaching class was given advice number 3, number 4, or number 5, and New Testament was given advice number 10, number 11, or number 12.

10. Advice number 6 was given for the Pastoral Care class, and advice number 2 was given for Overett's class.

11. Ethics has three textbooks fewer than Hyland's class, but Ethics has one textbook more than Cena's class.

12. Advice number 3 was not given to a Thursday class, advice number 7 was not given to a Tuesday class, and advice number 12 was given to a class with 5 textbooks.

13. Hyland and Keller do not have a Monday class, and they do not have class on the same day of the week.

14. Swinton's class is on Monday, and New Testament class is on Thursday.

15. Consider the Ethics class and the Teaching class: one is on Thursday, and one is taught by Overett.

16. The number of textbooks in Winters' and Paris's classes is the same.

17. Consider the Diaconal Ministry and Greek classes: one was given advice number 1, and one was given advice number 7.

18. Church History is a Thursday class, but it is not taught by Hyland. Hyland teaches a different Thursday class.

Grid for Seminary Class Schedule

	Albom	Cena	DiCamillo	Gutiérrez	Hyland	Keller	Miller	Overett	Paris	Swinton	Thornton	Winters	Monday	Monday	Monday	Tuesday	Tuesday	Tuesday	Wednesday	Wednesday	Wednesday	Thursday	Thursday	Thursday	2 Books	2 Books	3 Books	3 Books	4 Books	4 Books	5 Books	5 Books	6 Books	6 Books	7 Books	7 Books	Advice #1	Advice #2	Advice #3	Advice #4	Advice #5	Advice #6	Advice #7	Advice #8	Advice #9	Advice #10	Advice #11	Advice #12
Church History																																																
Diaconal Ministry																																																
Ethics																																																
Greek																																																
Hebrew																																																
New Testament																																																
Old Testament																																																
Pastoral Care																																																
Preaching																																																
Sacraments																																																
Teaching																																																
Theology																																																
Advice #1																																																
Advice #2																																					
Advice #3																																					
Advice #4																																					
Advice #5																																					
Advice #6																																					
Advice #7																																					
Advice #8																																					
Advice #9																																					
Advice #10																																					
Advice #11																																					
Advice #12																																					
2 Books																									
2 Books																									
3 Books																									
3 Books																									
4 Books																									
4 Books																									
5 Books																									
5 Books																									
6 Books																									
6 Books																									
7 Books																									
7 Books																									
Monday													
Monday													
Monday													
Tuesday													
Tuesday													
Tuesday													
Wednesday													
Wednesday													
Wednesday													
Thursday													
Thursday													
Thursday													

Hard Times

Recommended verses: See appendix
Difficulty: medium

Someday, God will restore the world and everyone in it. For now, the world is full of injustices, disappointments, diseases, and suffering. At times, it feels like our lives are falling apart, yet God is there. Even in pain, we can still find a bit of comfort in God. Sometimes, comfort is found by doing religious activities, like reading the Bible or taking communion. At other times, God brings us comfort through other people, like friends or support groups. There are times too when God brings us comfort through the gifts he has given us, such as the ability to create art or by volunteering.

Match the name of the person with his or her problem and the coping method.

Categories

Name: Alice, Bane, Charlotte, Elliot, Gwen, Kate, Louis, Malika, Oliver, Steve, Vito, and Yuki
Problem: cancer, death of a family member, discrimination, dying marriage, family member with dementia, going to prison, homelessness, infertility, joblessness, paralysis, poverty, and single and lonely
Coping method: attending a support group, communion, creating art, fasting, observing nature, prayer and mourning, quoting scriptures, reading the Bible, seeking a pastor's guidance, singing hymns, talking with a friend, and volunteering

Clues

1. The pain of a dying marriage is soothed by creating art.
2. Malika struggles with the death of a family member or a family member with dementia.
3. The pain of paralysis is soothed by attending a support group.
4. Vito is troubled by homelessness.
5. The pain of discrimination is dealt with by fasting.
6. Gwen is not going to prison, facing joblessness, or single and lonely, but she copes with her trouble by volunteering.
7. The pain of going to prison is soothed by communion.
8. Louis is not troubled by cancer, a family member with dementia, or poverty, but he copes with his trouble through prayer and mourning.
9. The pain of being single and lonely is soothed by quoting scriptures.
10. Bane struggles with a dying marriage or being single and lonely.
11. The pain of infertility is soothed by talking with a friend.
12. Yuki struggles with discrimination or infertility.
13. The pain of cancer is soothed by observing nature.
14. Oliver is not troubled by discrimination, infertility, or poverty, but he copes with his trouble by taking communion.
15. The pain of homelessness is soothed by singing hymns.
16. Alice talks with a friend, Charlotte reads the Bible, Elliot observes nature, and Kate quotes scriptures, but none of them are going to prison.
17. Steve is learning to live with paralysis, and Louis is struggling with the death of a family member.

Grid for Hard Times

	Alice	Bane	Charlotte	Elliot	Gwen	Kate	Louis	Malika	Oliver	Steve	Vito	Yuki	Attending Support Group	Communion	Creating Art	Fasting	Observing Nature	Prayer and Mourning	Quoting Scriptures	Reading Bible	Seeking Pastor's	Guidance	Singing Hymns	Talking with a Friend	Volunteering
Cancer																									
Death of a Family Member																									
Discrimination																									
Dying Marriage																									
Family Member with Dementia																									
Going to Prison																									
Homelessness																									
Infertility																									
Joblessness																									
Paralyzed																									
Poverty																									
Single and Lonely																									
Attending Support																									
Group																									
Communion																									
Creating Art																									
Fasting																									
Observing Nature																									
Prayer and Mourning																									
Quoting Scriptures																									
Reading Bible																									
Seeking Pastor's Guidance																									
Singing Hymns																									
Talking with a Friend																									
Volunteering																									

Hard Times: High School Edition

Recommended verses: See verses listed below
Difficulty: hard

High school is often a time of difficult transitions. Some of the problems listed below are usually experienced by someone in school. Other problems can be experienced by anyone at any age. Regardless, God is always there, helping people cope.

God helps people to cope through a variety of methods. Sometimes, he helps through religious practices, such as prayer and reading the Bible. At other times, God heals through moments of silence and reflection, such as prayer and journaling. Sometimes, he puts other people in a position of power for our benefit, like a counselor or doctor. In addition, God heals people by building relationships with friends, groups, and animals. God even uses the spiritual gifts given to us to help ourselves and others; two examples of this are tutoring and playing an instrument. Our God is a god of healing.

Categories

Name: Casey, Felicia, Hermione, Jévon, Ken, Lana, Monique, Nino, Olivia, Preston, Roxanne, Scarlet, Tyrelle, and Wally

Problem: autism, belief one is ugly, bullied at school, depression, eating disorder, end of relationship, failing classes, fighting with parents, grandparent died, moving, new stepparent, peer pressure to drink, unsure about future career, and worried about college

Coping method: attending a support group, attending a youth group, being a math tutor, going to a doctor, journaling, meeting with a tutor, playing an instrument, playing with the dog, prayer, reading the Bible, silent meditation, speaking with a counselor, taking a spiritual gifts test, and talking with a friend

Bible verse: 1 Corinthians 1:26–29, 1 Corinthians 6:19–20, 1 Corinthians 15:33, 2 Corinthians 1:3–4, Ephesians 6:1–3, Jeremiah 29:11, Joshua 1:9, Peter 3:3–4, Psalm 40:1–31, Psalm 147:3, 1 Philippians 4:6–7, Romans 12:19–20, Romans 13:7, and 1 Thessalonians 4:13–18

Clues

1. The person who is moving reads Joshua 1:9 and is Hermione or Lana.
2. Nino reads 1 Thessalonians 4:13–18 and plays with the dog, but Nino is not troubled by the belief that he is ugly.
3. The person who is autistic copes by being a math tutor.
4. Consider Casey, Felicia, and Wally: one is bullied at school, one copes by taking a spiritual gifts test, and one reads 1 Corinthians 1:26–29.
5. Consider Hermione, Jévon, and Ken: one is failing classes, one copes with silent meditation, and one reads Philippians 4:6–7.
6. Consider Lana, Monique, Nino: one believes that he or she is ugly, one has had a grandparent die, and one deals with peer pressure to drink.
7. Consider Olivia, Preston, and Roxanne: one has depression, one has an eating disorder, and one has a problem fighting with his or her parents.
8. Consider Scarlet, Tyrelle, and Wally: one copes by being a math tutor, one copes by playing an instrument, and one copes by reading the Bible.
9. Consider Psalm 40:1–3, Romans 12:19–20, and Romans 13:7: one is read by Felicia, one is read by Preston, and one is read by the person who is fighting with his or her parents.

10. Consider Casey, Jévon, and Roxanne: one is unsure about his or her future career, one is worried about college, and one copes with prayer.

11. Monique does journaling, Olivia goes to the doctor, and Wally is a math tutor.

12. The person who is at the end of a relationship enjoys reading the Bible, especially Psalm 147:3.

13. Romans 12:19–20 is read by the person who copes by attending a youth group, and this person is Felicia or Ken.

14. 1 Corinthians 6:19–20 is read by the person who goes to the doctor.

15. Ephesians 6:1–3 is read by the person with the new stepparent, which is Roxanne or Scarlet, and Jeremiah 29:11 is read by Casey or Wally.

16. The person feeling peer pressure to drink is soothed by speaking with a counselor.

17. Olivia does not have depression, and Preston does not read Romans 13:7.

18. Psalm 40:1–3 is read by the person who attends the support group to cope with his or her depression, and the person who is failing classes copes by meeting with a tutor.

19. The Bible verses are as follows: the verses read by Casey; Jévon; Nino; Scarlet; and Wally; the one for the person at the end of a relationship, the one for the person who is failing classes, the one for the person who copes by attending a support group, the one for the person who copes by attending a youth group, the one for the person who copes with prayer, 1 Corinthians 6:19–20, 1 Corinthians 15:33, Joshua 1:9, and 1 Peter3:3–4.

20. 1 Peter 3:34 is not read by the person who speaks with a counselor, 1 Corinthians 15:33 is not read by the person who fights with his or her parents, and Philippians 4:6–7 was not read by the person who is unsure about his or her future career.

21. Hermione reads Joshua 1:9.

Grid for Hard Times: High School Edition

	Casey	Felicia	Hermione	Jévon	Ken	Lana	Monique	Nino	Olivia	Preston	Roxanne	Scarlet	Tyrelle	Wally	Attending a support group	Attending youth group	Being a Math tutor	Going to a doctor	Journaling	Meeting with a tutor	Playing an instrument	Playing with the dog	Prayer	Reading Bible	Silent Meditation	Speaking with a counselor	Taking a spiritual gifts test	Talking with a friend	1 Corinthians 1:26-29	1 Corinthians 6:19-20	1 Corinthians 15:33	2 Corinthians 1:3-4	Ephesians 6:1–3	Jeremiah 29:11	Joshua 1:9	1 Peter 3:3-4	Philippians 4:6-7	Psalm 147:3	Psalm 40:1-3	Romans 12:19-20	Romans 13:7	1 Thessalonians 4:13-18
Autistic																																										
Believes he/she is ugly																																										
Bullied at school																																										
Depression																																										
Eating disorder																																										
End of relationship																																										
Failing classes																																										
Fighting with parents																																										
Grandparent died																																										
Moving																																										
New step-parent																																										
Peer-pressure to drink																																										
Unsure about future career																																										
Worried about college																																										
1 Corinthians 1:26-29																																										
1 Corinthians 6:19-20																																										
1 Corinthians 15:33																																										
2 Corinthians 1:3-4																																										
Ephesians 6:1–3																																										
Jeremiah 29:11																																										
Joshua 1:9																																										
1 Peter 3:3-4																																										
Philippians 4:6-7																																										
Psalm 147:3																																										
Psalm 40:1-3																																										
Romans 12:19-20																																										
Romans 13:7																																										
1 Thessalonians 4:13-18																																										
Attending a support group																																										
Attending youth group																																										
Being a Math tutor																																										
Going to a doctor																																										
Journaling																																										
Meeting with a tutor																																										
Playing an instrument																																										
Playing with the dog																																										
Prayer																																										
Reading Bible																																										
Silent Meditation																																										
Speaking with a counselor																																										
Taking a spiritual gifts test																																										
Talking with a friend																																										

Easter Egg Hunt

Recommended verses: See appendix
Difficulty: medium

Your church is having a series of Easter egg hunts for children of various ages. Each grade will search for a different number of eggs, in a separate location, with a different overseer.

Despite the preparations, many parents remain nervous about getting their kid(s) to the right place. You and your best friend are helping at the Easter egg hunt. Your friend writes down all of the information on a large white board. Use the clues to match the grade, the number of eggs, the location, and the overseer.

Categories

Grade: pre-K/kindergarten, first grade, second grade, third grade, fourth grade, and fifth grade
Number of eggs: 300, 325, 350, 375, 400, and 425
Location: Backyard, Fellowship Hall, Front Yard, Nursery, Playground, and Sunday School Room
Overseer: Miss Dahl, Miss Zander, Mr. Fry, Mr. Piper, Mr. Turner, and Mrs. Gardner

Clues

1. Fifth grade has twenty-five more eggs than fourth grade
2. Third grade has twenty-five fewer eggs than pre-K/kindergarten.
3. Miss Dahl's group has one hundred eggs more than fourth grade.
4. Mrs. Gardner's group has 300 eggs and is not in the backyard or the front yard.
5. Second grade is in the front yard, and fifth grade is in the backyard.
6. The grades are as follows: one is first grade, one is fifth grade, one has 425 eggs, one has Mr. Fry, one has Mrs. Gardner, and one is on the playground.
7. Miss Zander oversees pre-K/kindergarten or first grade in the Sunday School room.
8. Mr. Piper's group is in the nursery, and it has 400 or more eggs.
9. The front yard has fifty fewer eggs than the playground.
10. Mr. Turner's group has fewer eggs than the second graders.

Grid for Easter Egg Hunt

	Pre K/Kindergarten	1st Grade	2nd Grade	3rd Grade	4th Grade	5th Grade	Backyard	Fellowship Hall	Front yard	Nursery	Playground	Sunday School room	Mr. Fry	Mr. Piper	Mr. Turner	Miss. Dahl	Miss. Zander	Mrs. Gardner
300																		
325																		
350																		
375																		
400																		
425																		
Mr. Fry																		
Mr. Piper																		
Mr. Turner																		
Miss. Dahl																		
Miss. Zander																		
Mrs. Gardner																		
Backyard																		
Fellowship Hall																		
Front yard																		
Nursery																		
Playground																		
Sunday School room																		

Resurrection Eggs

Recommended verses: See appendix
Difficulty: medium

Resurrection eggs are an interactive way of teaching children about Jesus's death and resurrection. Twelve plastic Easter eggs are hidden with symbolic items inside. These items start the story on Palm Sunday, when Jesus rides into town on a donkey, and end it on Easter, after he has risen from the tomb.

Inside the eggs are the following:[5]

1. **A leaf:** Represents Palm Sunday, when Jesus rode into Jerusalem on a donkey and palms were laid at his feet.
2. **Dimes:** Represents the thirty pieces of silver Judas Iscariot received for betraying Jesus.
3. **A thimble:** Represents a cup at the Last Supper, before Jesus's death.
4. **A paper scroll:** Represents Jesus's prayer in the garden of Gethsemane.
5. **A piece of leather:** Represents Jesus being flogged.
6. **Twig crown:** Represents the crown of thorns the soldiers placed on Jesus's head.
7. **Nails:** Represents the nails that were hammered into Jesus to keep him on the cross.
8. **Dice:** Represents when the soldiers cast lots for Jesus's clothes.
9. **A broken toothpick:** Represents the spear that pierced Jesus's side.
10. **Soft fabric:** Represents the cloth that Jesus's body was wrapped in.
11. **A rock:** Represents the stone that was pushed in front of the tomb where Jesus was buried.
12. **Nothing:** Represents the empty tomb because Jesus came back to life after being dead for three days.

In this puzzle, twelve children have found one egg each with one item inside. Solve the puzzle to discover the name of the child who found the egg, the egg color, and the surprise inside.

Categories

Name: Armand, Blossom, Cassie, Doug, Ethan, Giselle, Keadra, Malachi, Roger, Sybil, Vadness, and Xavier
Color: black, blue, brown, gold, green, pink, orange, purple, red, silver, white, and yellow
Surprise inside: broken toothpick, dice, dimes, nothing, nails, leaf, paper scroll, piece of leather, rock, soft fabric, thimble, and twig crown

Clues:

1. Armand or Blossom finds the silver egg.
2. If Armand finds the silver egg, then it has a piece of leather in it.
3. If Blossom finds the silver egg, then it has a broken toothpick in it.
4. Giselle or Roger finds the red egg, and it has a paper scroll in it.
5. If the green egg has nails in it, then orange egg has nothing in it.
6. If the blue egg has nothing in it, then the purple egg was found by Sybil.
7. The yellow egg has soft fabric in it and was not found by Malachi, Roger, or Sybil.
8. The pink egg has a rock in it, and it was found by Cassie or Doug.
9. The black egg holds dice, the blue egg holds nails, the gold egg holds a twig crown, the purple egg holds nothing, and the white egg holds dimes.

---

[5] Ehman, Mandi. "DIY Resurrection Eggs & Easter Story Book Printables." Life Your Way. Accessed April 2016.

10. Armand's egg holds a thimble, Cassie's egg holds a twig crown, Ethan's egg holds a piece of leather, Roger's egg holds dimes, and Xavier's egg holds dice.

11. Malachi's egg is purple or orange, and Vadness has a blue egg.

12. If Keadra's egg is yellow, then the piece of leather is in the green egg.

13. The orange egg was not found by Ethan or Vadness.

14. If the leaf is in Blossom's egg, then the thimble is in the orange egg.

Grid for Resurrection Eggs

	Armand	Blossom	Cassie	Doug	Ethan	Giselle	Keadra	Malachi	Roger	Sybil	Vadness	Xavier	Broken Toothpick	Dice	Dimes	Leaf	Nails	Nothing	Paper Scroll	Piece of Leather	Rock	Soft Fabric	Thimble	Twig Crown
Black																								
Blue																								
Brown																								
Gold																								
Green																								
Orange																								
Pink																								
Purple																								
Red																								
Silver																								
White																								
Yellow																								
Broken Toothpick																								
Dice																								
Dimes																								
Leaf																								
Nails																								
Nothing																								
Paper Scroll																								
Piece of Leather																								
Rock																								
Soft Fabric																								
Thimble																								
Twig Crown																								

My Soul Sings to You

Recommended verses: See appendix
Difficulty: medium

Songs are powerful things. They share feelings and knowledge. They tell stories and relay messages. Singing to God connects you to him, regardless of what the song is about. If you have ever been to a church service, the odds are that you have heard at least one song. Maybe the song expressed what you wanted to say; maybe not. Church is not the only place to hear songs about God. Many artists have created modern versions of traditional church hymns, while others have created completely new songs.

The following puzzle is about ten Christians, their favorite traditional church hymns, and their favorite modern Christian songs.

Categories

Name: Alejandro, Claire, Jules, Latoya, Marvin, Perry, Sable, Theodore, Victoria, and Walter
Church hymn: "All Are Welcome," "America the Beautiful," "Away in a Manger," "Blessed Assurance," "I Am the Bread of Life," "Jesus Loves Me," "Nearer My God to Thee," "On Eagle's Wings," "Onward Christian Soldiers," and "Were You There …"

Modern Christian song:

- "Amazing Grace (My Chains Are Gone)" by Chris Tomlin
- "Awesome God" by Rich Mullins
- "Courageous" by Casting Crowns
- "Forgiveness" by Toby Mac
- "God's Not Dead" by Newboys
- "My Soul Will Rest" by MPK Christian Celtic Band
- "Overcomer" by Mandisa
- "Something about the Name Jesus" by Kirk Franklin
- "The Basin and the Towel" by Michael Card
- "Unbreakable" by Fireflight

Clues:

1. Consider Jules, Marvin, and Theodore: one favors the modern song "Awesome God," one favors the modern song "Overcomer," and one favors the traditional song "Were You There …."
2. If Latoya favors the traditional song "All Are Welcome," then Perry favors the traditional song "On Eagle's Wings."
3. If Claire favors the modern song "God's Not Dead," then Sable favors the modern song "Awesome God."
4. If Perry favors the traditional song "Away in a Manger," then Walter favors the traditional song "Nearer My God to Thee."
5. If Victoria favors the traditional "Jesus Loves Me," then Walter favors the modern "Amazing Grace (My Chains Are Gone)."
6. If Alexandro favors the modern song "Forgiveness," then Theodore favors the traditional song "Blessed Assurance."

7. Consider Alexandro, Sable, and Victoria: one favors the modern song "My Soul Will Rest," one favors the traditional song "On Eagle's Wings," and one favors the traditional song "Onward Christian Soldiers."

8. Perry favors the traditional song "America the Beautiful" or "I Am the Bread of Life."

9. "Unbreakable" is a modern song favored by the same person who favors the traditional song "On Eagle's Wings."

10. The person who favors the modern song "The Basin and the Towel" is not the same person who favors the traditional song "Nearer My God to Thee."

11. Consider Alejandro, Latoya, and Victoria: one favors the modern song "The Basin and the Towel," one favors the traditional song "Jesus Loves Me," and one favors the traditional song "On Eagle's Wings."

12. The person who favors the traditional song "America the Beautiful" favors the modern song "God's Not Dead."

13. Claire favors the modern song "Forgiveness," Theodore favors the traditional song "All Are Welcome," and Victoria favors the modern song "My Soul Will Rest."

14. "Overcomer" is favored by the same person who favors the traditional song "Nearer My God to Thee."

15. Consider Claire, Perry and Sable: one favors the modern song "Something about the Name Jesus," one favors the traditional song "America the Beautiful, and one favors the traditional song "I Am the Bread of Life."

16. Jules does not favor the traditional song "Were You There …," and Walter does not favor "Blessed Assurance."

Grid for My Soul Sings to You

	Alejandro	Claire	Jules	Latoya	Marvin	Perry	Sable	Theodore	Victoria	Walter	Amazing Grace (My Chains are Gone) by Chris Tomlin	Awesome God by Rich Mullins	Courageous by Casting Crowns	Forgiveness by Toby Mac	God's Not Dead by Newboys	My Soul will Rest by KMP Christian Celtic Band	Overcomer by Mandisa	Something about the Name Jesus by Kirk Franklin	The Basin and the Towel by Michael Card	Unbreakable by Fireflight
America the Beautiful																				
All are Welcone																				
Away in a Manger																				
Blessed Assurance																				
I am the Bread of Life																				
Jesus loves Me																				
Nearer my God to Me																				
On Eagle's Wings																				
Onward Christian Soldiers																				
Were You There…																				
Amazing Grace (My Chains are Gone)																				
Awesome God																				
Courageous																				
Forgiveness																				
God's Not Dead																				
My Soul will Rest																				
Overcomer																				
Something about the Name Jesus																				
The Basin and the Towel																				
Unbreakable																				

The Nine Soloists

Recommended verses: See appendix
Difficulty: easy

There's a benefit concert occurring today. Nine soloists are playing nine different instruments and nine different Christian songs. Use the clues to figure out who is playing what instrument and song.

Categories

Name: Axel, Dazhawn, Helen, Jericho, Lafayette, Madison, Nina, Otto, and Silver
Instrument: bells, clarinet, flute, guitar, piano, saxophone, trombone, trumpet, and violin
Song: "Here I Am, Lord," "How Great Thou Art," "It Is Well with My Soul," "Jesus Remember Me," "Ode to Joy," "One Bread, One Body," " Shout to the Lord," "Take My Life That I May Be," and "The Storm Is Passing Over"

Clues

1. Consider the bells and the piano: one was plated by Madison, and one played "Here I Am, Lord."
2. Dazhawn played "It Is Well with My Soul" but not on the clarinet, piano, or trumpet.
3. Lafayette played the flute or the saxophone, and the song was "One Bread, One Body" or "The Storm Is Passing Over."
4. The soloists are as follows: one was Dazhawn, one was Lafayette, one was Madison, one was Silver, one played the trombone, one played the violin, one played "Here I Am, Lord," one played "How Great Thou Art," and one played "The Storm is Passing Over."
5. "Ode to Joy" was played by Axel, but not on the violin.
6. "The Storm Is Passing Over" was played on the trumpet, but not by Helen or Otto.
7. Jericho played "Here I Am, Lord," Helen played "Take My Life, That I May Be," the clarinet player played "How Great Thou Art" and the bell player played "Jesus Remember Me."
8. "Shout to the Lord" was played on the saxophone by Silver or Lafayette.

Grid for The Nine Soloists

	Axel	Dazhawn	Helen	Jericho	Lafyette	Madison	Nina	Otto	Silver	Here I am Lord	How Great Thou Art	It is Well with my Soul	Jesus Remember Me	Ode to Joy	One Bread, One Body	Shout to the Lord	Take my Life, That I May Be	The Storm is Passing Over
Bells																		
Clarinet																		
Flute																		
Guitar																		
Piano																		
Saxaphone																		
Trombone																		
Trumpet																		
Violin																		
Here I am Lord																		
How Great Thou Art																		
It is Well with my Soul																		
Jesus Remember Me																		
Ode to Joy																		
One Bread, One Body																		
Shout to the Lord																		
Take my Life, That I May Be																		
The Storm is Passing Over																		

Spiritual Gifts: Romans 12:6–8

Recommended verses: See appendix
Difficulty: easy

You're a professor teaching a seminar on spiritual gifts, based on the passage in Romans 12:6–8. These are the spiritual gifts:[6]

1. **Exhortation.** To encourage and strengthen others.
2. **Giving.** To donate generously and for unselfish reasons.
3. **Leadership.** The ability to responsibility care for the needs of other people.
4. **Mercy.** Having compassion for those who are physically, mentally, emotionally, or spiritually suffering.
5. **Prophecy.** "The ability to receive a divinely inspired message and deliver it to others in the church."[7]
6. **Serving.** Being able to willingly and lovingly care for others. This might be the most diverse spiritual gift.
7. **Teaching.** Educating people, especially in matters of God and the Bible.

As the lesson ends, you ask the class to consider what their spiritual gifts may be and hand out an anonymous survey. The clues will show you how many people believe that they have been blessed with a particular spiritual gift. Match the spiritual gift with the number of votes.

Categories

Spiritual gift: exhortation, giving, leadership, mercy, prophecy, serving, and teaching
Number of votes: 2, 4, 5, 6, 7, 9, and 11

Clues

1. Only two people thought they may have the gift of prophecy.
2. The three most popular gifts were giving, leadership, and teaching.
3. More people believe they have the gift of mercy than the gift of exhortation.
4. The spiritual gifts with an even number of votes were prophecy, exhortation, and mercy.
5. The votes for the gift of leadership minus the votes for the gift of prophecy equals 7 votes.
6. The gift of teaching does not have 7 votes.

[6] "Spiritual Gifts Tests for Adult and Youth." Spiritual Gifts Test. Accessed July 27, 2016. https://spiritualgiftstest.com/
[7] Same as #6.

Grid for Spiritual Gifts: Romans 12:6–8

	2	4	5	6	7	9	11
Exhortation							
Giving							
Leadership							
Mercy							
Prophecy							
Serving							
Teaching							

Spiritual Gifts: 1 Corinthians 12:7–10

Recommended verses: See appendix
Difficulty: easy

A youth group is learning about the spiritual gifts mentioned in 1 Corinthians 12:7–10. The gifts are the following:[8]

1. **Distinguishing between spirits (also called "discernment")**. Having good judgment about a person, situation, idea, and so on.
2. **Faith**. Having great trust in God and godly matters.
3. **Healings**. The ability to occasionally heal others spiritually or physically.
4. **Interpretation of tongues**. The ability to translate messages spoken in tongues.
5. **Miracles**. A rare gift that allows for powerful, unusual, or impossible things to happen.
6. **Prophecy**. "The ability to receive a divinely inspired message and deliver it to others."[9]
7. **Tongues**. A gift of revelation from God, but it is usually in a nonhuman language.
8. **Words of knowledge**. Knowledgeable about God and capable of sharing this knowledge with others.
9. **Words of wisdom**. "It means to speak to the life of an individual or to a specific situation with great understanding and a righteous perspective, with the goal of guiding others toward a life of holiness and worship."[10]

Each youth asked a question about one of the spiritual gifts. Use the clues to match the name of the youth with the spiritual gift he or she asked about.

Categories

Spiritual gift: Distinguishing between spirits, faith, gifts of healings, interpretation of tongues, miracles, prophecy, tongues, words of knowledge, and words of wisdom
Name: Brandon, Crystal, Henry, Iesha, Josh, Richard, Sarah, Yvette, and Zelda

Clues

1. Zelda asked about distinguishing between spirits or healings.
2. Consider Crystal and Henry: one asked about faith, and one asked about prophecy.
3. Richard asked about tongues or the interpretation of tongues.
4. Consider Brandon, Sarah, and Zelda: one asked about tongues, one asked about healings, one asked about words of knowledge.
5. Iesha and Yvette did not ask about miracles, but one of them did ask about words of wisdom.
6. The spiritual gifts are as follows: the one Brandon asked about, the one Henry asked about, the one Sarah asked about, the one Yvette asked about, one was healings, one was interpretation of tongues, one was miracles, one was prophecy, and one was words of wisdom.
7. Josh asked about miracles, and Sarah did not ask about words of knowledge.

---

[8] Same as #6

[9] Same as #6

[10] Same as #6

Grid for Spiritual Gifts: 1 Corinthians 12:7–10

	Brandon	Crystal	Henry	Iesha	Josh	Richard	Sarah	Yvette	Zelda
Distinguishing Between Spirits									
Faith									
Healings									
Interpretation of Tongues									
Miracles									
Prophecy									
Tongues									
Word of Knowledge									
Word of Wisdom									

Spiritual Gifts: 1 Corinthians 12:28

Recommended verses: See appendix
Difficulty: medium

The tenth-grade youth group recently learned about the spiritual gifts listed in 1 Corinthians 12:28. These spiritual gifts are follows:[11]

1. **Apostleship.** The responsibility of sharing the Word of God with people who have never heard it and starting new churches.
2. **Administration.** The ability to help people or programs stay organized and reach their goals.
3. **Helps.** Being able to graciously relieve others.
4. **Miracles.** A rare gift that allows for powerful, unusual, or impossible things to happen.
5. **Kinds of healings.** The occasional ability to heal others spiritually or physically.
6. **Being a prophet (also known as the "gift of prophecy").** "The ability to receive a divinely inspired message and deliver it to others in the church."[12]
7. **Being a teacher (also known as "teaching").** Involves educating people, especially in matters of God and the Bible.
8. **Tongues.** A gift of revelation from God, but it is usually in a nonhuman language.

After the lesson, each youth told someone about their spiritual gift. Match the name of the person with the spiritual gift they mentioned and the person they talked to.

Categories

Names of youth: Autumn, Coral, Eddie, Jeremy, Lester, Misty, Stormie, and Wayne
Spiritual gift: apostle, administration, helps, kinds of healings, miracles, prophet, teacher, and tongues
Person they talked to: bus driver, coworker, father, friend, grandma, mailman, neighbor, and teammate

Clues

1. Coral talked to a teammate, but not about miracles or tongues.
2. Lester talked to his grandma, but not about administration or helps.
3. Stormie talked to a bus driver, but not about administration or miracles.
4. Jeremy talked to his father, but not about miracles or tongues.
5. Misty talked about apostleship or teachers to a friend or the mailman.
6. Autumn talked about prophets or teachers to a coworker or the mailman.
7. Wayne talked to a coworker or a friend or a neighbor.
8. Eddie did not talk about miracles or teachers, and he did not talk to a coworker.
9. The person who talked to a coworker did not talk about apostleship or miracles.
10. The person who talked about helps talked to his or her father or grandma.
11. The person who talked to a friend talked about prophets.
12. The person who talked about kinds of healings was not Lester or Stormie.
13. If Eddie talked to the mailman, then the person who spoke to his or her coworker talked about tongues.
14. If Wayne spoke to his coworker, then Autumn talked about prophets.
15. If the mailman heard about all kinds of healings, then the coworker heard about administration.

---

[11] Same as #6

[12] Same as #6

16. If Stormie talked about teachers, then the teammate heard about apostleship.
17. Grandma didn't learn about apostles or tongues, and the mailman didn't learn about miracles or tongues.
18. The neighbor learned about administration or apostleship.
19. The coworker did not hear about administration or kinds of healings.
20. Wayne talked to the mailman, or he talked about administration.

Grid for Spiritual Gifts: 1 Corinthians 12:28

	Autumn	Coral	Eddie	Jeremy	Lester	Misty	Stormie	Wayne	Bus driver	Co-Worker	Father	Friend	Grandma	Mailman	Neighbor	Teammate
Administration																
Apostle																
Helps																
Kinds of Healings																
Miracles																
Prophet																
Teacher																
Tongues																
Bus driver																
Co-Worker																
Father																
Friend																
Grandma																
Mailman																
Neighbor																
Teammate																

Christians Taking an Evolution Course

Recommended verses: See appendix
Difficulty: easy

An instructor is teaching a course on evolution. The instructor asks each student to write down on a piece of paper why he or she is taking the course. This instructor knows that at least five of the students in the class are Christians. Here are their reasons for taking the course:

1. **Reason 1:** "I can learn more about what I believe by understanding what I don't believe."
2. **Reason 2:** "Parts of evolution are compatible with Genesis."
3. **Reason 3:** "I want to be able to have intelligent conversations about both Christianity and evolution."
4. **Reason 4:** "This is a required class with no other options."
5. **Reason 5:** "My friends are taking this course."

Match the student with the reason he or she gave.

Categories

Name: Dennis, Jasmine, Lex, Mario, and Rose
Reason: 1, 2, 3, 4, and 5

Clues

1. Reason 1 was written by Dennis or Jasmine.
2. Reason 2 was written by Dennis or Lex.
3. Reason 4 was written by Mario or Rose.
4. Reason 4 was not written by Mario.
5. Reason 5 was written by Rose.
6. Lex did not write reason 2.

Grid for Christians Taking an Evolution Course

	Dennis	Jasmine	Lex	Mario	Rose
Reason 1					
Reason 2					
Reason 3					
Reason 4					
Reason 5					

Christian Men at Work

Recommended verses: See appendix
Difficulty: hard

Christians work in numerous places, doing a variety of things, with different groups of people. There is no single image of a Christian worker in secular society. The same is true about hobbies. Christians can have all kinds of interests. Have you ever wondered who in your life might be a Christian?

It started with a statement: "All Christians act the same. There is nothing unique or interesting about them."

Your response was, "What are you talking about? Christians are very different." You decide to prove this with a survey of twelve random men at your church. In the survey, you note their names, jobs, and hobbies. Solve the clues to put all of the information together.

Categories

Name: Alex, Buck, Dwayne, Forrest, Harrison, Jay, Kordell, Labron, Octavian, Ronald, Stephen, and Ulrich
Job: anthropologist, bookkeeper, certified nursing assistant, dad working at home, forklift driver, genealogist, illustrator, marriage counselor, painter, police officer, translator, and waiter
Hobby: cooking, fishing, gardening, jogging, playing hockey, playing with the grandkids, printmaking, reading, traveling, volunteering, watching crime shows, and weight lifting

Clues

1. The anthropologist likes playing hockey, the bookkeeper likes printmaking, and the marriage counselor likes fishing.
2. Consider Buck, Forrest, and Harrison: one is a dad working at home, one is a waiter, and one enjoys watching crime shows.
3. The forklift driver enjoys cooking, but is not Alex, Buck, Stephen, or Forrest.
4. Buck does not enjoy watching crime shows, Kordell does not enjoy volunteering, Octavian does not enjoy gardening, and Ronald does not enjoy fishing.
5. The men are as follows: one is Jay, one is Labron, one is Stephen, one is a dad working at home, one is a forklift driver, one is an illustrator, one is a marriage counselor, one is a police officer, one is a waiter, one likes playing hockey, one likes reading, and one likes watching crime shows.
6. Consider Alex, Forrest, and Stephen: one is a marriage counselor, one is a painter, and one enjoys volunteering.
7. Kordell enjoys reading, Stephen enjoys traveling, and Ulrich enjoys playing with the grandkids.
8. Consider Jay, Octavian, and Ronald: one is a forklift driver, one is a translator, and one enjoys jogging.
9. Dwayne enjoys playing hockey or printmaking, but he is not a genealogist or an illustrator.
10. The person who enjoys volunteering is not a waiter, and the person who enjoys playing with the grandkids is not a certified nursing assistant.
11. Consider Buck, Labron, or Ulrich: one is a police officer, one is a waiter, and one likes printmaking.
12. Consider the certified nursing assistant, the genealogist, and the translator: one enjoys reading, one enjoys watching crime shows, and one enjoys weight lifting.
13. Jay enjoys weight lifting, but Octavian does not enjoy jogging.
14. The certified nursing assistant does not like crime shows.

Grid for Christian Men at Work

	Alex	Buck	Dwayne	Forest	Harrison	Jay	Kordell	Labron	Octavian	Ronald	Stephen	Ulrich	Anthropologist	Bookkeeper	Certified Nursing Assistant	Dad working at home	Fork Lift Driver	Genealogist	Illustrator	Marriage Counselor	Painter	Police Officer	Translator	Waiter
Cooking																								
Fishing																								
Gardening																								
Jogging																								
Playing hockey																								
Playing with the grandkids																								
Printmaking																								
Reading																								
Traveling																								
Volunteering																								
Watching crime shows																								
Weight-lifting																								
Anthropologist																								
Bookkeeper																								
Certified Nursing Assistant																								
Dad working at home																								
Fork Lift Driver																								
Genealogist																								
Illustrator																								
Marriage Counselor																								
Painter																								
Police Officer																								
Translator																								
Waiter																								

Christian Women at Work

Recommended verses: See appendix
Difficulty: hard

Christians work in numerous places, doing a variety of things, with different groups of people. There is no single image of a Christian worker in secular society. The same is true about hobbies. Christians can have all kinds of interests. Have you ever wondered who in your life might be a Christian?

It started with a statement: "All Christians act the same. There is nothing unique or interesting about them."

Your response was "What are you talking about? Christians are very different." You decide to prove this with a survey of twelve random women at your church. In the survey, you note their names, jobs, and hobbies. Solve the clues to put all of the information together.

Categories

Name: Chaunsee, Darcy, Eve, Florette, Hadassah, Jewel, Myat, Nicole, Opal, Renee, and Sylvia
Job: accountant, clown, end-of-life counselor, graphic designer, jewelry designer, marketing strategist, military chaplain, mom working at home, ophthalmologist, paralegal, and screenwriter
Hobby: bowling, doll-making, drawing manga, making videos, playing video games, skydiving, social networking, stargazing, swimming, throwing parties, watching football, and zumba

Clues

1. If the ophthalmologist enjoys throwing parties, then the paralegal likes watching football.
2. If Florette likes bowling, then Myat is the graphic designer.
3. If Hadassah is a jewelry designer, then Renee is a pharmacist.
4. Chaunsee does not work at home, and Eve is not a graphic designer.
5. The accountant does not like stargazing, the clown does not like bowling, and the paralegal does not like swimming.
6. Sylvia is the end-of-life counselor or the military chaplain, and she enjoys drawing manga or playing video games.
7. The accountant is not Brooklyn, Myat, Nicole, or the person who likes making videos.
8. Florette is the screenwriter, and Jewel is the ophthalmologist.
9. The person who likes playing video games is the end-of-life counselor.
10. The mom working at home likes stargazing, but is not Brooklyn, Hadassah, or Opal.
11. The person who likes to zumba is the graphics designer.
12. The graphic designer is not Brooklyn, Hadassah, or Renee.
13. Consider Chaunsee, Darcy, and Eve: one is a jewelry designer, one is a marketing strategist and one is a paralegal.
14. Consider Opal, Renee, and Sylvia: one enjoys drawing manga, one enjoys playing video games, and one enjoys skydiving.
15. Eve enjoys making videos, but she is not a jewelry designer.
16. The clown enjoys skydiving, and the ophthalmologist enjoys throwing parties.
17. The women are as follows: one is Darcy, one is Eve, one is Nicole, one is Opal, one is a graphic designer, one is a jewelry designer, one is a military chaplain, one is a screenwriter, one enjoys skydiving, one enjoys social networking, one enjoys swimming, and one enjoys throwing parties.
18. The pharmacist does not like to swim.

Grid for Christian Women at Work

	Brooklyn	Chaunsee	Darcy	Eve	Florette	Hadassah	Jewel	Myat	Nicole	Opal	Renee	Sylvia	Bowling	Doll-making	Drawing Manga	Making videos	Playing video games	Skydiving	Social networking	Stargazing	Swimming	Throwing parties	Watching football	Zumba
Accountant																								
Clown																								
End-of-life Counselor																								
Graphic Designer																								
Jewelry Designer																								
Marketing Strategist																								
Military Chaplain																								
Mom working at home																								
Ophthalmologist																								
Paralegal																								
Pharmacist																								
Screenwriter																								
Bowling																								
Doll-making																								
Drawing Manga																								
Making videos																								
Playing video games																								
Skydiving																								
Social networking																								
Stargazing																								
Swimming																								
Throwing parties																								
Watching football																								
Zumba																								

Women of the Bible Presentations: Day 1

Recommended verses: See appendix
Difficulty: hard

Woman have often played important roles in the Bible. Some were prophetess, judges, faithful followers of God, loyal wives, caring mothers, the persuaders of kings, deceivers, and so on. God used women, not just men, to accomplish great things. The Bible really would really different without women in it.

A seminary class is giving presentations on women in the Bible. Match the name of the biblical woman with the name of the presenter and the grade the presenter earned. Here is a bit of information about the presented biblical women:

1. **Anna.** A prophetess who fasted, prayed, and worshiped at the temple. She prophesized about Jesus.
2. **Elizabeth.** An old, barren woman married to a priest named Zechariah. She gave birth to John the Baptist and confirmed that Mary was pregnant with the son of God.
3. **Esther.** A beautiful, young Jewish woman who married King Xerxes. God used her to save the Jewish people from annihilation.
4. **Jezebel.** Wife of King Ahab and worshipper of Baal. She attempted to kill the prophet Elijah, just as she had killed many other prophets.
5. **Leah.** Became the first wife of Jacob, because of her father's deception. Leah is described as being hated, but she gives birth to six sons and at least one daughter. Jesus descends from her bloodline.
6. **Lot's Daughters.** Lost their husbands, mother, and home when God destroyed Sodom. They got their father drunk and slept with him before giving birth to Moab, father of the Moabites, and Ben-Ammi, father of the Ammonites.
7. **Martha.** Had a sister named Mary and a brother named Lazarus. She was reprimanded for focusing on housework when Jesus came to visit but showed great faith after Lazarus died.
8. **Mary, the mother of Jesus.** A virgin who was engaged to Joseph when an angel told her that she would give birth to the son of God through the Holy Spirit. She prompts Jesus to do his first miracle at a wedding. She watched him die on the cross.
9. **Priscilla.** Wife of Aquila. They were tent makers Paul stayed with. Paul mentioned them for their faith in God and for the risks they took protecting him.
10. **Sarah.** Wife of Abraham and mother of Isaac. She was beautiful, yet barren, so gave her servant Hagar to her husband and regretted it. Also, she laughed at God for claiming she would have a child at age eighty, but she gave birth to Isaac.

Categories

Biblical woman: Anna, Elizabeth, Esther, Jezebel, Leah, Lot's Daughters, Martha, Mary, Priscilla, and Sarah
Name of presenter: Charity, Darius, Fifi, Gwenelle, Harper, Jordan, Maria, Sid, Tau, and Ulysses
Grade: A, A-, B+, B, B-, C+, C, C-, D, and F

Clues

1. The A and A- presentations were about Esther and Leah.
2. Gwenelle and Maria's reports were not a C+, C, C-, D, or F.
3. Tau's report was about Lot's daughter's, and Ulysses's report was about was about Elizabeth.

4. Consider Darius, Sid, and Ulysses: their grades were B+, C-, and F, but none of them did the presentations on Anna, Mary, or Martha.

5. Darius's presentation about Sarah received a lower grade than Harper's presentation, and Harper's presentation received a lower grade than the presentation about Anna.

6. The presentation on Priscilla received an F but was not given by Darius.

7. Consider the presentations on Esther, Jezebel, and Mary: one received an A-, one was done by Harper, and one was done by Maria.

8. Fifi did the report on Anna, which was a B+, B, or B-.

9. The presentation on Lot's daughters received a C.

10. Jezebel was not presented by Harper, and Leah was not presented by Jordan.

11. Fifi's grade was better than Jordan's but not as good as the person who presented on Jezebel.

12. Gwenelle presented on Leah.

Grid for Women of the Bible Presentations: Day 1

	Anna	Elizabeth	Esther	Jezebel	Leah	Lot's Daughters	Martha	Mary	Priscilla	Sarah	A	A-	B+	B	B-	C+	C	C-	D	F
Charity																				
Darius																				
Fifi																				
Gwenelle																				
Harper																				
Jordan																				
Maria																				
Sid																				
Tau																				
Ulysses																				
A																				
A-																				
B+																				
B																				
B-																				
C+																				
C																				
C-																				
D																				
F																				

Women of the Bible Presentations: Day 2

Recommended verses: See appendix
Difficulty: medium

Woman played many important roles in the Bible. Some were prophets, judges, faithful followers of God, loyal wives, caring mothers, the persuaders of kings, deceivers, and so on. God used women, not just men, to accomplish great things. The Bible would be really different without women in it.

A seminary class is giving presentations on women in the Bible. Match the name of the biblical woman with the name of the presenter and the grade the presenter earned. Here is a bit of information about the presented biblical women:

1. **Bathsheba.** Wife of King David, former wife of Uriah, and mother of Solomon. King David gets her pregnant and has her husband, Uriah, killed on the battlefield. Her first baby dies, but she later gives birth to Solomon, the future king.
2. **Deborah.** A wise woman, prophetess, and wife. She was one of the judges of Israel responsible for fighting against idolatry in the land. Deborah sent for Barak to join her in war against the Canaanites.
3. **Eve.** The first woman, first wife, first mother, first person to be tempted, first human to sin, and the first parent to bury a child. She and Adam lived in the Garden of Eden until banished.
4. **Gomer.** Hosea's wife. God told Hosea to marry a promiscuous woman, to parallel the relationship between God and Israel. Gomer had at least three children, and at least one of them was not Hosea's. Gomer runs off with a lover and ends up in slavery, but Hosea buys her back.
5. **Lydia.** A merchant who sells purple cloth. She already believes in God when Paul arrives. After hearing Paul, she had her entire household baptized and persuaded Paul and Silas to stay at her house.
6. **Mary Magdalene.** Jesus removed seven demons from her. She faithfully followed Jesus, even observing his crucifixion after the disciples had fled. She was one of the women who testified about Jesus's resurrection.
7. **Miriam.** Sister of Aaron and Moses, and a prophetess. She watched baby Moses on the Nile and spent many years as a slave in Egypt. Miriam briefly suffered from leprosy after she challenged Moses's leadership.
8. **Queen of Sheba.** A wise queen who came from far away to test the knowledge of Solomon. She asked many questions. Though she offered him many gifts, Solomon sent her away with more than she arrived with.
9. **Rahab.** A prostitute who risked her life to save some Israelite spies. She persuaded the spies to spare her and her household. She gives birth to Boaz, whose descendant is Jesus.
10. **Samaritan Woman.** An outcast on the edge of society who married five times. She had a conversation with Jesus about living water. Many Samaritans believed in Jesus because of her testimony.

Categories

Biblical woman: Bathsheba, Deborah, Eve, Gomer, Lydia, Mary Magdalene, Miriam, Rahab, Ruth, and the Samaritan Woman
Name of presenter: Ace, Bonita, Cheryl, Horatio, Jillian, Omar, Precious, Stanley, Tod, and Wren
Grade: A, A-, B+, B, B-, C+, C, C-, D, and F

Clues

1. The biblical women are as follows: one is Bathsheba, one is Deborah, one is Eve, one is presented by Ace, one is presented by Bonita, one is presented by Precious, one is presented by Stanley, one earned a C+, one earned a C, and one earned a C-.

2. The grades are as follows: one earned on the Deborah presentation, one earned on the Gomer presentation, one earned on the Samaritan woman presentation, one earned by Cheryl, one earned by Wren, the A-, the B, the B-, the C-, and the F.

3. Jillian did not earn an A or A-; Horatio did not earn a B+, B, or B-; Omar did not earn a C+, C, or C-; and Tod did not earn a D or F.

4. The person who presented on Mary Magdalene earned an A-, the person who presented on Ruth earned a B, the person who presented on Rahab earned a C+, and the person who presented on Eve got a D.

5. Horatio presented Bathsheba, Omar presented Deborah, and Stanley presented Gomer.

6. Consider Ace and Tod: one presented on Miriam, and one presented on Ruth.

7. Bonita's grade is higher than the person who did Lydia.

8. The presentation Gomer earned a B+ and the presentation on Miriam earned a C-.

9. Omar's grade is higher than Bonita's and Cheryl's grade is lower than Wren's.

Grid for Women of the Bible Presentations: Day 2

	Ace	Bonita	Cheryl	Horatio	Jillian	Omar	Precious	Stanley	Tod	Wren	A	A-	B+	B	B-	C+	C	C-	D	F
Bathsheba																				
Deborah																				
Eve																					
Gomer																					
Lydia																					
Miriam																					
Mary Magdalene																					
Rahab																					
Samaritan woman																					
Ruth																					
A																				
A-																				
B+																				
B																				
B-																				
C+																				
C																				
C-																				
D																				
F																				

Parables from Jesus

Recommended verses: See appendix
Difficulty: medium

Parables are lessons told in story form. Jesus often taught in parables; this was partly because it was easier to remember stories than lessons. Also, parables left room for mysteries in Jesus's messages. Jesus didn't like to answer questions straightforwardly.

The second grade Sunday school class is learning about parables. The students are voting to determine which parables will be discussed over the next few weeks. Match the name of the person who suggested the parable with the title of the parable and the number of votes the parable got.

Categories

Name: Blair, Hailey, Rhianna, Scott, Takao, Ursula, and Violet
Parable: the evil farmers, the farmer scattering seeds, the fishing net, the lost sheep, the ten bridesmaids, the three servants, and the unforgiving debtor
Number of Votes: 1, 2, 3, 4, 5, 6, and 7

Clues

1. The parable of the farmer scattering seeds received three more votes than the parable Violet suggested.
2. The votes for the parable of the evil farmers plus the votes for the parable of the fishing net equals the number of votes that Takao's suggested parable received.
3. The parable of the lost sheep was not suggested by Blair, Hailey, Scott, or Ursula.
4. The parable of the unforgiving debtor was suggested by Rhianna, Scott, or Takao and received 1 or 4 votes.
5. The parable of the ten bridesmaids was recommended by Hailey and received fewer than 4 votes.
6. The votes for the parable of the three servants minus the votes for Violet's suggested parable equals the number of votes for the parable of the unforgiving debtor.
7. Takao's suggested parable received 6 votes, and Blair's suggested parable got 5 votes.
8. The parable of the fishing net got more votes than the parable of the evil farmers but fewer votes than the lost sheep.
9. Neither Blair nor Violet suggested the evil farmers and neither Hailey nor Rhianna suggested the unforgiving debtor.
10. Scott's suggested story received fewer votes than Violet's.
11. Rhianna's suggested story received more votes than Ursula's.

Grid for Parables by Jesus

	Blair	Hailey	Rhianna	Scott	Takao	Ursula	Violet	1	2	3	4	5	6	7
The Evil Farmers														
The Farmer Scattering Seeds														
The Fishing Net														
The Lost Sheep														
The Ten Bridesmaids														
The Three Servants														
The Unforgiving Debtor														
1														
2														
3														
4														
5														
6														
7														

Saints and Martyrs

Recommended verses: See appendix

Difficulty: easy

The term "saint" is defined as "a person who is officially recognized by the Christian church as being very holy because of the way he or she lived."[13] Some saints are even considered to have been involved in miracles. In the Catholic church, there are days to honor certain saints. The term "martyr" is defined as "a person who is killed or who suffers greatly for a religion, cause, etc."[14] Martyrs are not people who want to die but people who were killed because they would not abandon their religious beliefs and conform to overall culture There are still places in today's world where Christians are killed for practicing their beliefs.

These Christians have each purchased the trading card of a saint or martyr from a shop. Match the name of the person with the saint or martyr on their card. Here is some information about the saints and martyrs:

1. **Drogo.**[15] He was an orphaned in early adulthood. He sold his property, became a pilgrim, and traveled to Rome nine times. Supposedly, Drogo could bilocate (be in two places at once). For forty years, he lived as a hermit.

2. **Elizabeth of Hungary.**[16] She was a Hungarian princess who married German Prince Ludwig and was thrown out after her husband died. Elizabeth served as a Franciscan nun until she died at age twenty-four. She is considered the saint of bakers, beggars, lace makers, and widows.

3. **Esther John.**[17] She was born in India as Qamar Zia on October 14, 1929. Her family moved to Pakistan, and she ran away to avoid marriage. She changed her name to Esther John and started working at an orphanage. In September 1956, Esther attended the United Bible Training Centre. She evangelized to Pakistani woman working in the cotton fields.

4. **Gerard Majella.**[18] He was born in poverty to a widowed mother in Italy. Gerard is said to have had the mystical gifts of bilocation, healing, and prophecy. Died at twenty-nine years old due to tuberculosis. Gerard is considered the patron saint of motherhood.

5. **Jan Hus.**[19] He was born a peasant in Husinec (Czech Republic); he earned a doctorate to become a preacher. Jan Hus wanted to protect the traditions of the church but also reform clergy and increase the power of church councils. He rebelled against the selling of indulgences (papers that forgive sins). On July 6, 1415, Jan Hus was burned at the stake.

---

[13] "Dictionary by Merriam-Webster: America's most-trusted online dictionary." Merriam-Webster. Accessed July 29, 2016. https://www.merriam-webster.com/.

[14] Same as #13

[15] "Saint Drogo." CatholicSaints.Info. May 12, 2016. Accessed August 9, 2016. https://catholicsaints.info/saint-drogo/.

[16] Mulvihill, Margaret, and David Hugh. Farmer. *The treasury of saints and martyrs*. New York: Viking, 1999. Page 47

[17] "Esther John." Westminster Abbey ". 2016. Accessed August 10, 2016. http://www.westminster-abbey.org/our-history/people/esther-john.

[18] Online, Catholic. "St. Gerard Majella - Saints & Angels." Catholic Online. 2016. Accessed August 10, 2016. http://www.catholic.org/saints/saint.php?saint_id=150.

[19] Tomkins, Stephen. "John Hus, Reforner Of Bohemia." Christian History Institute. Accessed August 03, 2016. https://www.christianhistoryinstitute.org/study/module/hus/.

6. **Joan of Arc.**[20] She was a peasant girl who at age thirteen started hearing the voices of the angel Michael, Saint Catherine of Andrea, and Saint Margaret of Antioch. At age nineteen, she led troops into battle and drove back the English. At a later battle, she was captured in battle and sold to the English, who burned her at the stake.

7. **Nicholas Ridley.**[21] He was born around 1503 in Northumbria (northern United Kingdom/ southeast Scotland.) He was a Protestant theologian, a master at Pembroke College, and a bishop of both Rochester and London. Queen Mary, a devout Catholic, had him declared a heretic and executed on October 16, 1555.

8. **Óscar Arnulfo Romero y Galdámez.** He was born in El Salvador on August 15, 1917. He was a conservative man who saw corruption in the government. He gave popular radio sermons and became archbishop of San Salvador. On March 24, 1980, he was assassinated in a chapel by members of a government death squad.

9. **Perpetua.**[22] She was a pregnant noblewoman who lived in North Africa during the time of the Roman Empire. Perpetua was imprisoned for being a Christian and refusing to sacrifice to the Roman emperor. Perpetua gave birth shortly before being sent to the arena. She survived attacks by a bull and a leopard but died by the sword of a Roman soldier.

10. **Polycarp of Smyrna.**[23] He was a second-century Christian since childhood, who was martyred at age eighty-six. He became the bishop of Smyrna (Turkey) despite having very little education. He argued against Gnosticism (the belief that Jesus's spirit came back after the resurrection, but not his body). During his arrest, Polycarp received a vision and understood that he was going to die. He was later tried and burned at the stake.

Categories

Name: Candace, Fern, Havana, Isadore, Jessica, Mikey, Shawn, Turquoise, Wilson, and Xun

Saint or martyr on card: Drogo, Elizabeth of Hungary, Esther John, Gerard Majella, Jan Hus, Joan of Arc, Nicholas Ridley, Óscar Arnulfo Romero y Galdámez, Perpetua, and Polycarp of Smyrna

Clues

1. If Shawn's card is Drogo, then Fern's card is Joan of Arc.
2. If Shawn's card is Elizabeth of Hungary, then Isadore's card is Polycarp of Smyrna.
3. If Shawn's card is Joan of Arc, then Wilson's card is Gerard Majella.
4. If Shawn's card is Esther John, then Xun's card is Perpetua.
5. If Shawn's card is Polycarp of Smyrna, then Havana's card is Nicholas Ridley.
6. If Jessica's card is Drogo, then Havana's card is Esther John.
7. If Turquoise's card is Drogo, then Candace's card is Nichols Ridley.
8. Consider Havana, Mikey, and Xun: they have the cards for Elizabeth of Hungary, Esther John, and Jan Hus.

[20] Same as #16. Pages 62-63

[21] Trueman, C.N. "Nicholas Ridley." History Learning Site. 2016. Accessed September 07, 2016. http://www.historylearningsite.co.uk/tudor-england/nicholas-ridley/.

[22] "Perpetua." Christian History | Learn the History of Christianity & the Church. 2016. Accessed September 13, 2016. http://www.christianitytoday.com/history/people/martyrs/perpetua.html.

[23] "Polycarp." Christian History | Learn the History of Christianity & the Church. 2016. Accessed September 13, 2016. http://www.christianitytoday.com/history/people/martyrs/perpetua.html.

9. Candace's card is not Joan of Arc, Turquoise's card is not Nicholas Ridley, and Mikey's card is not Jan Hus.

10. Shawn's card is Elizabeth of Hungary, Joan of Arc, or Polycarp of Smyrna.

11. Elizabeth of Hungary is the card of Mikey or Xun.

12. Jessica's card is Óscar Arnulfo Romero y Galdámez.

13. Consider Fern and Isadore: their cards are Perpetua and Polycarp of Smyrna.

14. Xun's card is Esther John and Wilson's card is Gerard Majella.

Grid for Saints and Martyrs

	Candace	Fern	Havana	Isadore	Jessica	Mikey	Shawn	Turquoise	Wilson	Xun
Drogo										
Elizabeth of Hungary										
Esther Jonh										
Gerard Majella										
Jan Hus										
Joan of Arc										
Nicholas Ridley										
Óscar Arnulfo Romero y Galdámez										
Perpetua										
Polycarp of Smyrna										

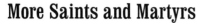

More Saints and Martyrs

Recommended verses: See appendix
Difficulty: medium

The term "saint" is defined as "a person who is officially recognized by the Christian church as being very holy because of the way he or she lived."[24] Some saints are even considered to have been involved in miracles. In the Catholic church, there are days to honor certain saints. The term "martyr" is defined as "a person who is killed or who suffers greatly for a religion, cause, etc."[25] Martyrs are not people who want to die but people who were killed because they would not abandon their religious beliefs and conform to overall culture There are still places in today's world where Christians are killed for practicing their beliefs.

These Christians have each purchased the trading card of a saint or martyr from a shop. Match the name of the person with the saint or martyr on their card. Here is some information about the saints and martyrs:

1. **Ambrose of Milan.**[26], [27] He had eloquent speaking skills and practiced law. The common citizens of Milan elected him bishop, even though he wasn't running. Ambrose adopted an ascetic lifestyle, wrote several important papers, and excommunicated Theodosius I.
2. **Charles de Foucauld.**[28] He was an orphaned aristocrat raised by his grandfather. He temporarily joined the French army. He also lived in a Trappist monastery for twenty-one years. Later, he started a religious community in Algeria and ended up writing Tuareg-French dictionaries and poetry.
3. **Francis Xavier.**[29] He joined the Jesuits. As a missionary, he traveled to India, Sri Lanka, and Malay. In Japan, he converted an abandoned Buddhist monastery and attracted a following of two thousand Japanese Christians within two years. He died on a voyage to China.
4. **Josephine Bakhita.**[30] At seven years old, she was captured in Sudan and sold into slavery. Bought by the Michieli family in Italy, Bakhita went to school with their daughter. She became Catholic, was baptized, and changed her name to Josephine. A court declared Josephine a free woman. She graduated from the Institute of St. Magdalene of Canossa and served in Schio, Italy.
5. **Margaret of Cortona.**[31] Born in Tuscany to farmers, she left home after her mother died. She lived with a man named Arsenio for nine years and gave birth to his son. Arsenio was murdered, so she moved in with her son. She became a Franciscan tertiary who regularly practiced prayer, penitence, and self-denial.

---

[24] Same as #13

[25] Same as #13

[26] "St. Ambrose." CATHOLIC ENCYCLOPEDIA: St. Ambrose. 1905. Accessed August 11, 2016. http://www.newadvent.org/cathen/01383c.htm.

[27] "Ambrose." Wikipedia. 2016. Accessed August 11, 2016. https://en.wikipedia.org/wiki/Ambrose.

[28] Miller, OFM Fr. Don. "Blessed Charles de Foucauld." Franciscan Media. Accessed August 11, 2016. https://www.franciscanmedia.org/blessed-charles-de-foucauld/

[29] Same as #16 Pages 66–67.

[30] Miller, OFM Fr. Don. "Saint Josephine Bakhita." Franciscan Media. 2016. Accessed August 11, 2016. https://www.franciscanmedia.org/saint-josephine-bakhita/.

[31] Miller, OFM Fr. Don. "St. Margaret of Cortona." Franciscan Media. 2016. Accessed August 11, 2016. https://www.franciscanmedia.org/saint-margaret-of-cortona/. *AmericanCatholic.org*. Web. 11 Aug. 2016.

6. **Nicholas of Myra.**[32] He was born in Patara (Turkey) to wealthy Christian parents before being orphaned. He was generous, loved children, and cared for sailors. Supposedly, Nicholas saved a poor man's daughters from slavery by paying their wedding dowries. (He threw bags of money in through the window, which landed in shoes and stockings.)

7. **Our Lady of Guadalupe.**[33] Roman-Catholic name of the Virgin Mary. In a legend from Guadalupe, Mexico City, she appeared to Juan Diego and sent him to the bishop. Juan's uncle became ill, but she told Juan that the uncle will recover. Mary put roses in Juan's tilma for the bishop, but when the roses were taken out, her image appeared.

8. **Thomas à Beckett.**[34] Henry II made Thomas the archbishop of Canterbury. Henry wanted church leaders to submit to his rule, but Thomas believed that the church should only submit to God. Henry II got drunk and ordered Thomas's death. The knights killed Thomas in the Canterbury Chapel. He is the patron saint of Portsmouth and officials.

9. **Veronica Giuliani.**[35] She was born in Italy, and at age seventeen, she convinced her father to allow her to become a nun. She joined the Poor Clares (the Order of Saint Clare), where she served in the infirmary, kitchen, and sacristy. At age thirty-seven, a stigmata appeared on her. At age sixty-five, she became an abbess (head of a nunnery) and remained one until her death.

Categories

Name: Arlene, Clark, Desmond, Kathleen, Fritz, Pennelope, Olander, Ubon, and Yolanda

Saint or martyr on card: Ambrose of Milan, Charles de Foucauld, Francis Xavier, Josephine Bakhita, Margaret of Cortona, Nicholas of Myra, Our Lady of Guadalupe, Thomas à Beckett, and Veronica Giuliani

Clues

1. If Arlene's card is Charles de Foucauld, then Desmond's card is Thomas à Beckett.
2. If Clark's card is Our Lady of Guadalupe, then Ubon's card is Francis Xavier.
3. If Kathleen's card is Josephine Bakhita, then Yolanda's card is Ambrose of Milan.
4. If Fritz's card is Nicholas of Myra, then Penelope's card is Ambrose of Milan.
5. If Olander's card is Francis Xavier, then Yolanda's card is Charles de Foucauld.
6. If Ubon's card is Charles de Foucauld, then Olander's card is Margaret of Cortona.
7. The Thomas à Beckett card belongs to Clark or Ubon.
8. The Josephine Bakhita card is not owned by Arlene, Desmond, Kathleen, or Pennelope.
9. The Our Lady of Guadalupe card belongs to Arlene or Olander.
10. The Veronica Giuliani card is not owned by Clark, Kathleen, Pennelope, or Ubon.
11. The Francis Xavier card belongs to Kathleen or Olander.
12. Arlene owns the Margaret of Cortona card, and Ubon owns Thomas à Beckett.
13. Fritz owns the Charles de Foucauld card or the Nicholas of Myra card.
14. The Charles de Foucauld card belongs to Desmond.

[32] "Who is St. Nicholas?" St. Nicholas Center. Accessed August 11, 2016. http://www.stnicholascenter.org/pages/who-is-st-nicholas/.

[33] Miller, OFM Fr. Don. "Our Lady of Guadalupe." Franciscan Media. 2016. Accessed August 11, 2016. https://www.franciscanmedia.org/our-lady-of-guadalupe/.

[34] Same as #16 Pages 52–53.

[35] Miller, OFM Fr. Don. "Saint Veronica Giuliani." Franciscan Media. 2016. Accessed August 11, 2016. https://www.franciscanmedia.org/saint-veronica-giuliani/.

Grid for More Saints and Martyrs

	Ambrose of Milan	Charles De Foucauld	Francis Xavier	Josephine Bakhita	Margaret of Cortona	Nicholas of Myra	Our Lady of Guadalupe	Thomas Beckett	Veronica Giuliani
Arlene									
Clark									
Desmond									
Kathleen									
Fritz									
Pennelope									
Olander									
Ubon									
Yolanda									

Plagues of Egypt

Recommended verses: See appendix

Difficulty: easy

When Pharaoh refused to let the Israelites sacrifice to God on a mountain, God sent plagues down into Egypt. These plagues did more than create chaos. Each plague was chosen to discredit one or more Egyptian gods. Here are some of the discredited Egyptian gods:[36]

1. **Plague of blood:** Mocks Hapi.
2. **Plague of frogs:** Mocks Heqet.
3. **Plague of gnats (Lice):** Mocks Geb.
4. **Plague of flies:** Mocks Khepri.
5. **Plague of livestock:** Mocks Amon, Bat, Hathor, and several others.
6. **Plague of festering boils:** Mocks Isis
7. **Plague of hail:** Mocks Nut
8. **Plague of locusts:** Mocks Osiris and Senehem.
9. **Plague of darkness:** Mocks Ra and Horus.
10. **Death of the firstborn son:** Mocks Pharaoh, who was seen as a god, and all other gods.

The message of the God of Israel is this: I am the one true God.

Next week's Sunday school lesson is on the plagues of Egypt. Ten people will give a short summary about each plague. Match each plague with the name of the person who will summarize it.

Categories

Plague: blood, darkness, death of the firstborn son, festering boils, flies, frogs, gnats, hail, livestock, and locusts

Name: Billy, Dominique, Joyce, Maureen, Naomi, Pamela, Sylvester, Vyra, Walter, and Zane

Clues

1. If Joyce summarizes the plague of gnats, then Walter summarizes the plague of locusts.
2. If Zane summarizes the plague of locusts, then Joyce summarizes the plague of blood.
3. If Vyra summarizes the plague of darkness, then Billy summarizes the plague of hail.
4. The plague of festering boils is not going to be summarized by Billy, Naomi, or Walter.
5. Vyra will summarize the plague of darkness, gnats, or livestock.
6. Sylvester will not summarize the plague of blood, festering boils, frogs, gnats, or locusts.
7. Dominique will summarize the plague of blood, the death of the firstborn son, or hail.
8. Maureen or Pamela will summarize the death of the firstborn son.
9. Consider the plagues of blood, frogs, and livestock: the summarizers are Naomi, Sylvester, and Walter.
10. Consider the plagues of darkness and locusts: the summarizers are Joyce and Pamela.
11. Pamela will summarize the plague of locusts.
12. The plague of frogs is not summarized by Naomi

---

[36] Isenhoff, Michelle. "Egyptian gods and the Ten Plagues." The Book and the Author. August 06, 2012. Accessed July 3, 2016. https://shellsstory.wordpress.com/2012/06/03/1821/.

Grid for Plagues of Egypt

	Billy	Dominique	Joyce	Maureen	Naomi	Pamela	Sylvester	Vyra	Walter	Zane
Blood										
Darkness										
Death of the Firstborn Son										
Festering Boils										
Flies										
Frogs										
Gnats										
Hail										
Livestock										
Locusts										

Happy Birthday, Baby!

Recommended verses: See appendix
Difficulty: hard

Having a baby is a unique experience. It is a relief for the parent(s) that the baby is finally here after nine months of pregnancy (or a long period of adoption). It is frightening yet wonderful to have such a small human being in your hands and in your care. A baby is one of the ways that God can bless a person, so birthdays are a reason to celebrate.

These twelve Christian families gave birth to twelve babies over the past year. Match the month, day of the week, and time the baby was born with the name of the baby.

Categories

Month: January, February, March, April, May, June, July, August, September, October, November, and December
Name: Belle, Elmyra, Faith, Gerald, Isaac, Jenny, Milo, Océane, Rufus, Titus, Uma, and Xander
Day of the week: Sunday (1), Monday (2), Tuesday (2), Wednesday (2), Thursday (2), Friday (2), and Saturday (1).
Time: 12:07 a.m., 2:45 a.m., 3:09 a.m., 5:02 a.m., 8:38 a.m., 11:24 a.m., 12:37 p.m., 1:15 p.m., 4:36 p.m., 6:05 p.m., 7:13 p.m., and 9:55 p.m.

Clues

1. Elmyra was born on a Thursday, Friday, or Saturday, and it was after 11:24 a.m.
2. Isaac was born more than three months after Jenny, but Isaac was born at an earlier time.
3. Titus was not born on Sunday, Tuesday, Thursday, or Friday.
4. Xander was born in January, February, or March; Faith was born in April, May, or June; Milo was born in July, August, or September; and Gerald was born in October, November, or December.
5. Consider Milo and Titus: one was born at 12:07 a.m., and one was born at 12:37 p.m.
6. Belle was born before 8:38 a.m., but Isaac was not.
7. There is a three-month difference between the birth of Elmyra and Rufus.
8. The times of birth are as follows: the time of the February baby, the time of the May baby, the time of the November baby, the time of Elmyra's birth, the time of Océane's birth, the time of Rufus' birth, 12:07 a.m., 3:09 a.m., 5:02 a.m., 12:37 p.m., 1:15 p.m., and 9:55 p.m.
9. Consider the people born on Thursday: one was born in September, and one was born at 2:45 a.m.
10. Isaac was born on a Tuesday in March or June; Uma was born at 9:55 p.m. on a Monday or Thursday.
11. Belle was born at least four months before Océane and at an earlier time.
12. The March baby was not born at 8:38 a.m., the July baby was not born at 9:55 p.m., the October baby was not born at 2:45 a.m., and the December baby was not born at 1:15 p.m.
13. The Sunday baby was not Faith, Jenny, Milo, or Rufus.
14. The January baby was born on a Wednesday at 12:37 p.m., the March baby was born on Saturday before 8:38 a.m., the April baby was born on Monday at 2:45 a.m. or 3:09 a.m., and the July baby was born between 4:36 p.m. and 9:55 p.m.
15. Consider Elmyra, Faith, and Gerald: each of them was born on a different day of the week. Also, one was born in July, one was born on Monday, and one was born at 2:45 am.

16. Jenny's time of birth was later than the time of birth for the baby born in December.

17. Jenny, and Océane were not born on Thursday; however, Faith was.

18. The Friday babies were born at 11:24 a.m. and 7:13 p.m.

19. The baby born at 6:05 p.m. was not born on Monday or Wednesday.

20. Gerald's time of birth was before Titus'.

Grid for Happy Birthday, Baby!

	January	February	March	April	May	June	July	August	September	October	November	December	12:07 AM	2:45 AM	3:09 AM	5:02 AM	8:38 AM	11:24 AM	12:37 PM	1:15 PM	4:36 PM	6:05 PM	7:13 PM	9:55 PM	Sunday	Monday	Monday	Tuesday	Tuesday	Wednesday	Wednesday	Thursday	Thursday	Friday	Friday	Saturday
Belle																																				
Elmyra																																				
Faith																																				
Gerald																																				
Issac																																				
Jenny																																				
Milo																																				
Océane																																				
Rufus																																				
Titus																																				
Uma																																				
Xander																																				
Sunday																																						
Monday																																						
Monday																																						
Tuesday																																						
Tuesday																																						
Wednesday																																						
Wednesday																																						
Thursday																																						
Thursday																																						
Friday																																						
Friday																																						
Saturday																																						
12:07 AM																																					
2:45 AM																																					
3:09 AM																																					
5:02 AM																																					
8:38 AM																																					
11:24 AM																																					
12:37 PM																																					
1:15 PM																																					
4:36 PM																																					
6:05 PM																																					
7:13 PM																																					
9:55 PM																																					

Nineteen Ways to Describe God

Recommended verses: See verses listed below
Difficulty: medium

Take a few minutes to write down as many words as you can to describe God. Now ask yourself, "Why did I describe God like that?" People use their own views of the world to decide who God is. Sometimes, this is a problem because humans view the world differently, and views about the world are constantly changing. God is consistent; he doesn't change. Fortunately, the Bible tells us a lot about God.

In this puzzle, you will use the clues to match the description of God to its corresponding Bible verse.

Categories

Description: biggest thing out there, faithful, father, impartial, jealous, judge, king of the earth, lion, love, merciful, mother, mysterious, omnipotent, omnipresent, omniscient, perfect, protector of orphans and widows, righteous, and rock

Bible verse: 1 Corinthians 8:6, 1 Corinthians 10:13, Deuteronomy 4:23–24, Deuteronomy 10:17, Deuteronomy 32:4, Ephesians 2:4–5, Hosea 11:10, Isaiah 26:4–5, Isaiah 66:1, Isaiah 66:13, 1 John 4:16, Job 11:7–9, Psalm 18:30, Psalm 47:7, Psalm 68:5, Psalm 76:7–10, Psalm 139:7–8, and Revelation 19:6

Clues

1. Psalm 47:7 identifies God as the king of the earth.
2. Hosea 11:10 identifies God as being like a lion or like a rock.
3. Job 11:7–9 identifies God as faithful or mysterious.
4. The verse that shows God is love is 1 John 4:16.
5. Consider 1 Corinthians 10:13, Deuteronomy 10:17, and Isaiah 66:13: each verse shows God as either faithful, impartial, or a mother.
6. Deuteronomy 32:2 identifies God as righteous.
7. God is shown as merciful in Deuteronomy 4:23–24, Ephesians 2:4–5, or Psalm 76:7–10.
8. Psalm 68:5 shows God as a protector of widows and orphans or as perfect.
9. God is identified as a father in 1 Corinthians 8:6, Psalm 18:30, or Romans 11: 33–35.
10. Romans 11:33–35 identifies God as omniscient.
11. Isaiah 66:13 shows God as love or as a mother.
12. Psalm 18:30 shows God as perfect.
13. God is shown to be the biggest thing out there in Isaiah 66:1 or Psalm 139:7–18.
14. Consider Isaiah 26:4–5 and Revelation 19:6: one shows God as omnipotent, and one shows God as a rock.
15. Psalm 76:7–10 shows God as a judge.
16. Deuteronomy 4:23–24 identifies God as jealous.
17. If Psalm 18:30 is the verse about God being perfect, then Psalm 139:7–18 is the verse about God being omnipresent.
18. If Hosea 11:10 is about God being like a lion, then Deuteronomy 10:17 is about God being impartial.
19. The verse about God being like a rock is found in Isaiah."

Grid for Nineteen Ways to Describe God

	1 Corinthians 10:13	1 Corinthians 8:6	Deuteronomy 4:23-24	Deuteronomy 10:17	Deuteronomy 32:4	Ephesians 2:4-5	Hosea 11:10	Isaiah 26:4-5	Isaiah 66:1	Isaiah 66:13	Job 11:7-9	1 John 4:16	Psalm 18:30	Psalm 47:7	Psalm 68:5	Psalm 76:7-10	Psalms 139:7-18	Revelation 19:6	Romans 11: 33-35
Biggest thing out there																			
Faithful																			
Father																			
Impartial																			
Jealous																			
Judge																			
King of the Earth																			
Lion																			
Love																			
Merciful																			
Mother																			
Mysterious																			
Omnipotent																			
Omnipresent																			
Omniscient																			
Prefect																			
Protector of orphans and widows																			
Righteous																			
Rock																			

Prophetic Books of the Bible

Recommended verses: Anything from the listed books
Difficulty: hard

The prophetic books of the Bible are more commonly known as the major and minor prophets. The minor prophets record prophetic events with less severe consequences or future prophetic events. These books are Amos, Habakkuk, Haggai, Hosea, Joel, Jonah, Malachi, Micah, Nahum, Obadiah, Zechariah, and Zephaniah. In contrast, the major prophets are books where the predicted events are already happening. These books are Daniel, Ezekiel, Isaiah, Jeremiah, and Lamentations. Please note that though there are only seventeen prophetic books, there over a hundred people who prophesized at one point or another in the Bible.

Below is a list of twelve students. Each student is researching a different minor prophet but working in a group to research a major prophet. The major prophet groups are two and three in size. Match each student with the minor and major prophet they are researching.

Categories

Name: Angelica, Bennett, Connie, Donald, Hugo, Irma, Judy, Mystelle, Rusty, Satoshi, Tyrone, and Vivian

Minor prophet: Amos, Habakkuk, Haggai, Hosea, Joel, Jonah, Malachi, Micah, Nahum, Obadiah, Zechariah, and Zephaniah

Major prophet: Daniel (2), Ezekiel (3), Isaiah (2), Jeremiah (3), and Lamentations (2)

Clues

1. Hugo, Judy, and Satoshi are all working in different groups on their major prophet.
2. Amos is being done by a person who is in the group researching Jeremiah.
3. Rusty is researching Haggai or Malachi and is in the group for Isaiah or Lamentations.
4. The major prophet group that Hugo is in has three people in it, but the group Angelica is in has two people.
5. Nobody in the Daniel group is doing Hosea, Micah, Obadiah, or Zephaniah.
6. Hugo and Tyrone don't get along, so they are not in the same group.
7. Neither Angelica nor Connie are in the Isaiah group, and Irma is not in the Lamentations group.
8. Consider the people who are researching the major prophet Ezekiel: one is Donald, one is Vivian, and one is the person researching the minor prophet Nahum.
9. The person who is doing Obadiah is not in the Lamentations group.
10. Tyrone is researching Hosea and is in the Jeremiah or Lamentations group.
11. Connie and Irma are working on the same major prophet.
12. Bennett is researching Micah, Judy is researching Nahum, and Satoshi is researching Habakkuk.
13. The people who are researching Jonah, Obadiah, and Zephaniah are not in the Jeremiah group.
14. Consider Hugo, Irma, and Mystelle: they are researching Haggai, Joel, and Zechariah. Also, two of the three are in the same major prophet group.
15. Donald is doing Obadiah, and Irma is doing Joel.
16. Mystelle is in the Isaiah group, and she is not researching Haggai.
17. The person who is researching Micah is not in Lamentations.

Grid for Prophetic Books of the Bible

	Angelica	Bennett	Connie	Donald	Hugo	Irma	Judy	Mystelle	Rusty	Satoshi	Tyrone	Vivian	Daniel	Daniel	Ezekiel	Ezekiel	Ezekiel	Isaiah	Isaiah	Jeremiah	Jeremiah	Jeremiah	Lamentations	Lamentations
Amos																								
Habakkuk																								
Haggai																								
Hosea																								
Joel																								
Jonah																								
Malachi																								
Micah																								
Nahum																								
Obadiah																								
Zechariah																								
Zephaniah																								
Daniel																								
Daniel																								
Ezekiel																								
Ezekiel																								
Ezekiel																								
Isaiah																								
Isaiah																								
Jeremiah																								
Jeremiah																								
Jeremiah																								
Lamentations																								
Lamentations																								

Baptisms

Recommended verses: See appendix
Difficulty: medium

Google defines "baptism" as "the religious rite of sprinkling water onto a person's forehead or of immersion in water, symbolizing purification or regeneration and admission to the Christian Church."[37]

Baptism is not limited to children; anyone can become baptized at any age. Jesus was about thirty years old when he was baptized. Though Jesus, God's Son, was sinless, he was baptized anyway; this pleased the Father, and the Holy Spirit descended upon Jesus. Baptism, which symbolizes death of a selfish, earthly life and the start of a new life in God, is done to Jesus as an example for other believers. Today, baptism is also a promise between the congregation and family of the baptized to assist the newly baptized as he or she grows in faith.

Ten Christians were baptized today. Match the name of baptized person with his or her age, the number of friends and family members standing beside the altar, and the name of church that held the baptism ceremony.

Please note that the names of the following churches are fictional.

Categories

Name: Brogan, Elodie, Gary, Hayden, Ivy, Marita, Raine, Sakura, Quint, and Terrance
Age: 2 months, 8 months, 5 years old, 10 years old, 15 years old, 29 years old, 38 years old, 40 years old, 62 years old, and 78 years old
Number of family and friends: 1, 2, 3, 4, 5, 7, 8, 10, 12, and 16
Church: Anointed, Back to the Bible, Calvary, Community of the Cross, First Assembly, Good Samaritan, Lakeside, Main Street, Second Coming, and Trinity

Clues

1. If Terrance is 8 months old, then Gary attends Community of the Cross.
2. If the person who is 38 years old goes to Second Coming, then the person who is 78 years old goes to Anointed.
3. Consider Elodie, Hayden, and Quint: one is baptized at Lakeside, one is 40 years old, and one had 5 friends at his or her baptism.
4. Marita is 15, 29, 38, or 62 years old, and she had 10 friends at her baptism.
5. The person with 1 friend at his or her baptism is 62 years old.
6. When Terrance is baptized, he is older than Elodie, but younger than Gary, and he does not attend Anointed, First Assembly, Good Samaritan, or Main Street.
7. Sakura is baptized at Anointed, Back to the Bible, or Calvary, and she was more than 38 years old when baptized.
8. The person who attends Second Coming is Marita or Quint.
9. The person who is baptized at Good Samaritan had 7 friends attend.
10. Consider Brogan, Raine, or Terrance: one is 78 years old, one is baptized at Main Street, and one is baptized at Trinity. Also, the number of friends is 3, 12, and 16.

---

[37] Google. Web. 30 July 2016.

11. The person who has 2 friends at his or her baptism is 29 years old.

12. Gary is baptized at First Assembly, Raine is baptized at Anointed, and Quint is baptized at Back to the Bible.

13. Quint is less than 5 years old when he is baptized, but Ivy is more than 15 years old when she is baptized.

14. Consider the 8-month-old, the 5-year-old, and the 15-year-old: one is Brogan, one is Elodie, and one attends First Assembly.

15. The person who has 7 friends at their baptism attends Good Samaritan.

16. The number of Terrance's friends minus nine equals the number of friends Brogan has at his baptism.

17. The 5-year-old is baptized at Lakeside with 8 friends.

Grid for Baptisms

	Brogan	Elodie	Gary	Hayden	Ivy	Marita	Quint	Raine	Sakura	Terrance	Anointed	Back to the Bible	Calvary	Community of the Cross	First Assembly	Good Samaritan	Lakeside	Main Street	Second Coming	Trinity	1	2	3	4	5	7	8	10	12	16
2 months																														
8 months																														
5 years old																														
10 years old																														
15 years old																														
29 years old																														
38 years old																														
40 years old																														
62 years old																														
78 years old																														
1																														
2																														
3																														
4																														
5																														
7																														
8																														
10																														
12																														
16																														
Anointed																														
Back to the Bible																														
Calvary																														
Community of the Cross																														
First Assembly																														
Good Samaritan																														
Lakeside																														
Main Street																														
Second Coming																														
Trinity																														

Jesus's Original Twelve Disciples

Recommended verses: See appendix
Difficulty: easy

To clarify, Jesus had more than twelve disciples. The word "disciple" means "student," so anyone who is seeking to learn and live in the will of God is a disciple of Jesus. The original twelve disciples are a significant part of Jesus's ministry. One of the twelve, Judas Iscariot, would betray Jesus to the Pharisees, leading to Jesus's death on the cross. The other eleven apostles, plus Paul, spread the good news about Jesus across Asia and Europe after Jesus ascended. Most of the people who learned about Jesus during that time period were influenced by the apostles' testimonies.

Your church is doing a play about Jesus's original twelve disciples. Auditions are held to decide who will get what part. After the auditions are over, you are given the sheet with the results to post.

Match the name of the person with the disciple he or she will be playing.

Categories

Name: Adele, Cole, D'Ante, Gordon, Hubert, Jim, Luther, Max, Roark, Teagan, Valmont, and Wade
Disciple: Andrew, Bartholomew (Nathanael), James (the Elder), James (the Younger), John, Judas, Jude (Thaddeus), Matthew (Levi), Peter (Simon Peter), Philip, Simon (the Zealot), and Thomas

Clues

1. Teagan acts as James (the Younger) or Judas.
2. D'Ante acts as Bartholomew (Nathanael), Matthew (Levi), or Thomas.
3. Hubert acts as Andrew or Philip.
4. Roark acts as Andrew, James (the Elder), or Thomas.
5. Adele acts as Jude (Thaddeus) or Peter (Simon Peter).
6. Wade acts as John or Philip.
7. Cole acts as James (the Elder) or James (the Younger).
8. Luther acts as Bartholomew (Nathanael) or Judas.
9. Valmont acts as John or Thomas.
10. Gordan acts as Peter (Simon Peter) or Simon (the Zealot).
11. Max acts as Matthew (Levi) or Simon (the Zealot).
12. Jim acts as Judas and Valmont acts as Thomas.

Grid for Jesus's Original Twelve Disciples

	Andrew	Bartholomew (Nathanael)	James (the Elder)	James (the Younger)	John	Judas	Jude (Thaddeus)	Matthew (Levi)	Peter (Simon Peter)	Philip	Simon (the Zealot)	Thomas
Adele												
Cole												
D'Ante												
Gordon												
Hubert												
Jim												
Luther												
Max												
Roark												
Teagan												
Valmont												
Wade												

Depression and Hope

Recommended verses: See verses listed below
Difficulty: easy

Ryan has been suffering from depression for a while now. He has been trying to take care of himself. He goes to the doctor and counselor regularly. He tries to take good care of his body by eating well, going for occasional walks, taking his medicine on time, and getting enough sleep. Still, it is very hard being depressed, and, sometimes, Ryan has relapses. A friend recommended that he read a few Bible verses, just in case it helped. Ryan decided to try, but reads just one verse a day.

Can you match the verse with the day that it is read?

Categories

Day: day 1, day 2, day 3, day 4, day 5, day 6, day 7, day 8, day 9, day 10, day 11, and day 12
Bible verse: Deuteronomy 31:8, Deuteronomy 32:10, Ecclesiastes 9:4, John 3:16–17, Matthew 5:3, Philippians 13, Philippians 4:6–8, Proverbs 3:5–6, Psalm 34:18, Psalm 40:1–3, Psalm 42:11, and Psalm 43:5

Clues

1. Deuteronomy 31:8, Matthew 5:3, and Psalm 43:5 are read on even-numbered days.
2. Philippians 13, Psalm 40:1–3, and Psalm 42:11 are read on odd-numbered days.
3. Ecclesiastes 9:4 was read two days before Psalm 34:18.
4. Proverbs 3:5–6 was read five days after Psalm 43:5.
5. Psalm 34:18 is read on day 3, and Psalm 40:1–3 is read on day 11.
6. John 3:16–17 is read after day 8.
7. Psalm 34:18 is read seven days before Deuteronomy 32:10.
8. Consider days 5, 6, and 12: the scriptures for those days are John 3:16–17, Matthew 5:3, and Psalm 42:11.
9. Philippians 13 was read on day 9, but Deuteronomy 31:8 was not read on day 4.
10. Psalm 43:5 was read on day 2

Grid for Depression and Hope

	Day 1	Day 2	Day 3	Day 4	Day 5	Day 6	Day 7	Day 8	Day 9	Day 10	Day 11	Day 12
Deuteronomy 31:8												
Deuteronomy 32:10												
Ecclesiastes 9:4												
John 3:16-17												
Matthew 5:3												
Philippians 4:6-8												
Philippians 13												
Proverbs 3:5-6												
Psalm 34:18												
Psalm 40:1-3												
Psalm 42:11												
Psalm 43:5												

Party Time

Recommended verses: See appendix
Difficulty: medium

There are a lot of parties mentioned in the Bible. When the Ark of God was brought back to Jerusalem, people celebrated and King David danced. Queen Esther established the festival of Purim because of how God helped her and Mordecai save the Jews from total annihilation. Even Jesus performed his first recorded miracle at a wedding. Parties are not a problem, unless they dishonor God. King Belshazzar had his party guests drink out of goblets from the temple of God, so a disembodied hand wrote his doom on the wall.

Categories

Host or Hostess: Bart, Dustin, Gigi, Hannah, Jamar, Koji, Reno, Stephanie, Tamara, and Zamari
Type of party: bachelor party, bachelorette party, birthday party, college acceptance party, dinner party, game night party, graduation, housewarming party, themed party, and wine-tasting party
Date: May 3, May 5, May 7, May 10, May 11, May 14, May 18, May 25, May 26, and May 31

Clues

1. If Koji is having the bachelor party, then Tamara is having the housewarming party.
2. If Reno is having the wine-tasting party, then Koji is having the birthday party.
3. If Stephanie is having the game night party, then the party's date will be May 26.
4. If Stephanie is having the graduation party, then the party's date will be May 11.
5. If the housewarming party is on May 14, then the bachelorette party is on May 25.
6. If the graduation party is on May 10, then the themed party is on May 26.
7. The bachelor party is hosted by Dustin, Koji, or Reno.
8. May 3 is the bachelor party, May 26 is the game night party, and May 31 is the wine-tasting party.
9. The gradation party is Dustin's or Tamara's, and the date is after Bart's college acceptance party.
10. The date of Koji's party is after Jamar's party but before Zamari's.
11. Here is the list of parties: Bart's party, Dustin's party, Gigi's party, Stephanie's party, the dinner party, the housewarming party, the themed party, the party on May 10, the party on May 25, and the party on May 31.
12. Consider Bart, Hannah, and Reno: one is having the college acceptance party, one is having the themed party, and one is having the wine-tasting party. Also, none of them are having parties on May 5, May 10, or May 25.
13. The bachelorette party is hosted by Gigi or Zamari.
14. Jamar's party is on May 5 or May 18, and it is not the birthday party.
15. Hannah's party is the themed party or the party on May 26.
16. The bachelorette party is on May 11, and Zamari's party is on May 18.
17. The themed party is after the housewarming party but before the college acceptance party.

Grid for Party Time

	Bachelor Party	Bachelorette Party	Birthday Party	College Acceptance Party	Dinner Party	Game Night Party	Graduation Party	Housewarming Party	Themed- Party	Wine Tasting Party	3-May	5-May	7-May	10-May	11-May	14-May	18-May	25-May	26-May	31-May
Bart																				
Dustin																					
Gigi																					
Hannah																					
Jamar																					
Koji																					
Reno																					
Stephanie																					
Tamara																					
Zamari																					
3-May																					
5-May																					
7-May																					
10-May																					
11-May																					
14-May																					
18-May																					
25-May																					
26-May																					
31-May																					

To Be Loved and To Love

Recommended verses: See verses listed below
Difficulty: medium

"For the past few weeks, we have been discussing love as defined in the Bible," says your teacher. "Here is the final assignment: First, you must pick a verse about love and write a three-hundred-word summary explaining the verse. Second, you must take a camera and snap a picture of biblical love in the world. Biblical love is not easily photographed, so be prepared to explain how this picture represents biblical love. The picture you take does not need to be related to the verse you summarize. This project is due the next time we meet. Class dismissed."

At the next class session, these were the pictures that had been taken:
1. A family of birds
2. Strangers eating lunch together in a park
3. Two hands holding each other
4. A young man raking an old woman's yard
5. A racial reconciliation meeting
6. People supporting each other in a three-legged race
7. The gravestone of a fallen soldier
8. A mother dog adopting pups that are not hers
9. Two young children sharing a toy

Use the clues to discover the name of the student, the verse he or she summarized, and the picture he or she took.

Categories

Name: Brock, Chin-Hwa, Herberto, Jojo, Kyran, Marty, Nadia, Shelby, and Warren
Verse: 1 Corinthians 13:1–13, John 15:13, John 13:34–35, 1 John 4:9–12, 1 John 4:19–21, Mark 12:29–31, Matthew 5:43–48, Psalm 91:14–16, and Romans 8:37–39
Picture: 1, 2, 3, 4, 5, 6, 7, 8, and 9

Clues

1. Kyran summarized 1 John 4:9–12, and Marty summarized 1 Corinthians 13:1–13.
2. The verses are as follows: Jojo's verse, Marty's verse, John 15:13, 1 John 4:19–21, Matthew 5:43–48, the verse with picture 1, the verse with picture 4, the verse with picture 7, and the verse with picture 8.
3. Herberto summarized John 15:13 or Psalm 91:14–16.
4. Picture 7 was taken by the person who summarized Mark 12:29–31.
5. Picture 4 was taken by Kyran or Warren.
6. Consider John 15:13, Matthew 5:43–48, Psalm 91:14–16: one is paired with Warren, one is paired with picture 5, and one is paired with picture 9.
7. Brock did not summarize Psalm 91:14–16, Nadia did not summarize John 15:13, Shelby did not summarize John 13:34–35, and Warren did not summarize Matthew 5:43–48.
8. Shelby took picture 1 or 2, Warren took picture 3 or 4, Jojo took picture 5 or 6, and Nadia took picture 7, 8, or 9.
9. Consider pictures 5, 7, and 9: they were taken by Brock, Herberto, and Nadia.

10. Romans 8:37–39 was done by the person who took picture 1.
11. The pictures are as follows: the picture taken by Brock, the picture taken by Chin-Hwa, the picture taken by Kyran, 1 Corinthians 13:1–13, John 13:34–35, Mark 12:29–31, picture 2, picture 4, and picture 9.

Grid for To Be Loved and To Love

	1 Corinthians 13:1-13	John 15:13	John 13:34-35	1 John 4:9-12	1 John 4:19-21	Mark 12:29-31	Matthew 5:43-48	Psalm 91:14-16	Romans 8:37-39	#1	#2	#3	#4	#5	#6	#7	#8	#9
Brock																		
Chin-Hwa																		
Herberto																		
Jojo																		
Kyran																		
Marty																		
Nadia																		
Shelby																		
Warren																		
#1																		
#2																		
#3																		
#4																		
#5																		
#6																		
#7																		
#8																		
#9																		

How to Be Beautiful

Recommended verses: See verses listed below
Difficulty: easy

In a circle sat eight high school girls. Four of them wore name-brand clothes. Five of them wore their hair in elaborate styles. Six of them wore makeup.

"I remember high school well," said the lecturer, sliding into chair beside the young women. "Makeup was a big thing at my high school. So was body shape, height, weight, hair color, and having the right clothes, which went out of style within a season. Young women who were not seen as beautiful were taught to envy other young women who spent all their time and money chasing after the approval of others.

"What the Bible tells us about beauty is so dramatically different from what our culture tells us. According to the Bible, God made us to be beautiful. Also, part of beauty is the way we treat ourselves and each other."

As the session ends, the lecturer passes around a box full of hand mirrors. Each young woman takes a hand mirror and chooses one Bible verse to write across the top of its frame. Match the names of the young women with the Bible verses and the mirror colors.

Categories

Name: Amity, Chona, Ginger, Heather, Kimiko, Marissa, Savannah, and Zibiah
Verse: Ecclesiastes 3:11, Genesis 1:27, John 7:24, 1 Peter 3:3–4, Proverbs 31:30, Psalm 139:13–16, 1 Samuel 16:7, and 1 Timothy 4:8
Color: black, brown, green, maroon, pink, teal, white, and yellow

Clues

1. Consider Amity and Ginger: they chose the verses 1 Samuel 16:7 and 1 Timothy 4:8. They do not have the yellow or black hand mirrors.
2. Consider Heather and Kimiko: they chose the verses Proverbs 31:30 and Psalm 139:13–16. They do not have the green or white hand mirrors.
3. The person with the maroon hand mirror wrote Psalm 139:13–1 on it, and the person with the white hand mirror wrote 1 Peter 3:3–4 on it.
4. Savannah did not write John 7:24 or 1 Timothy 4:8, but Ginger wrote one of them.
5. The black hand mirror belongs to Kimiko or Zibiah, and the teal hand mirror belongs to Chona or Marissa.
6. 1 Peter 3:3–4 is not on the hand mirror belonging to Chona or Zibiah.
7. Heather owns the maroon hand mirror, and Zibiah owns the pink hand mirror.
8. Ecclesiastes 3:11 is on the yellow hand mirror.
9. Genesis 1:27 or 1 Timothy 4:8 is on the brown hand mirror.
10. If Heather has the teal hand mirror, then Marissa wrote John 7:24 on her hand mirror.
11. If Genesis 1:27 was written by Savannah, then Ginger owns the green hand mirror.
12. The hand mirror with Ecclesiastes 3:11 written on it belongs to Chona.

Grid for How to Be Beautiful

	Ecclesiastes 3:11	Genesis 1:27	John 7:24	1 Peter 3:3-4	Proverbs 31:30	Psalm 139:13-16	1 Samuel 16:7	1 Timothy 4:8	Black	Brown	Green	Maroon	Pink	Teal	White	Yellow
Amity																
Chona																
Ginger																
Heather																
Kimiko																
Marissa																
Savannah																
Zibiah																
Black																
Brown																
Green																
Maroon																
Pink																
Teal																
White																
Yellow																

Kings and Queens

Recommended verses: See appendix
Difficulty: hard

Kings and queens played important roles in the Bible. The actions of those who ruled affected whether the Israelites followed God or not. Moreover, the actions of kings and queens largely impacted the future in positive or negative ways.

1. **Ahab.** Husband of Queen Jezebel. He sacrificed two of his sons to Baal. Ahab coveted Naboth's vineyard. Ahab's actions resulted in a drought predicted by the prophet Elijah.
2. **Asa.** Third king of Judah. He removed idols from Judah. With God's help, Asa defeated the Cushites and King Baasha. Asa became oppressive later in life and developed a foot disease.
3. **Cyrus.** Also called Cyrus the Great. He was the king of Persia. God used him to end the Jews' captivity in Babylon. Cyrus ordered that the temple in Jerusalem be rebuilt, and he sent money and sacred objects back to the temple.
4. **Esther.** Was born Hadassah. Esther was a Jewish orphan who lived with her cousin, Mordecai. She was taken away and married King Xerxes, which made her the queen of Persia. God used Esther to save the Jews from total annihilation. Esther established the festival of Purim.
5. **Herod Agrippa.** Married Herodias, despite the warnings of John the Baptist. Herod had John the Baptist and James (disciple of Jesus) executed, and he imprisoned Peter. An angel made him deathly ill after Herod made an arrogant speech.
6. **Nebuchadnezzar.** He ruled the Babylonian empire, destroying Judah and capturing its residents. He dreamed about a statue made of gold, silver, bronze, and clay. He had Shadrach, Meshach, and Abednego thrown into a blazing furnace for not bowing to his statue. Also, Nebuchadnezzar temporarily went insane for seven years.
7. **Pharaoh.** Technically a title rather than a name. I am referring to the pharaoh Moses and Aaron spoke to. Pharaoh's heart was hardened by God, and Egypt was struck with plagues. Pharaoh released the Israelites, only to chase them across the Red Sea, causing his soldiers to drown.
8. **Queen of Sheba.** A wise queen who came from far away to test the knowledge of Solomon. She asked many questions. Though she offered him many gifts, Solomon sent her away with more than she arrived with.
9. **Rehoboam.** The son of Solomon, who did not listen to the advice of his elders. He taxed the Israelites even more harshly than his father did. This split the kingdom into two, with only the tribe of Judah staying loyal to Rehoboam.
10. **Saul.** The first king of Israel. Originally, he did not want to be king. After disobeying God, Saul was told that he would lose his kingship. Saul repeatedly tried to kill David to keep him from becoming king. After Saul sought the Witch of Endor, the ghost of the prophet Samuel revealed that Saul would die in battle the next day.
11. **Solomon.** The second son of King David and Bathsheba. He asked God for wisdom and was rewarded with power and wealth too. He married over seven hundred women, which caused him to worship foreign gods. He built the temple in Jerusalem.
12. **Vashti.** The wife of King Xerxes. She refused to come to him at a banquet to show off her beauty before all of the male guests. King Xerxes banished Vashti and replaced her with Esther.

The sixth grade mentors are working with their first grade mentees to prepare two pages for a book. A king or queen is randomly assigned to each mentor and mentee. Together they must draw a picture

and write a paragraph about their king or queen. When they are finished, they give their pages to the teacher, and the pages are bound together in a book. The table of contents lists the page number, the name of the king or queen, the name of the sixth grade mentor, and the name of the first grade mentee. Use the clues to figure out what the contents says.

Categories

Page number: 2, 4, 6, 8, 10, 12, 14, 16, 18, 20, 22, and 24

Kings and queens: Ahab, Asa, Cyrus, Esther, Herod Agrippa, Nebuchadnezzar, Pharaoh, Queen of Sheba, Rehoboam, Saul, Solomon, and Vashti

Sixth grade mentor: Adam, Barry, Chris, Freddie, Gabby, Hasan, J'waun, Kiki, Margaret, Pearl, Tahoma, and Vladimir

First grade mentee: Angel, Bella, Cynthia, Drake, Humphrey, Joseph, June, Lief, Ming, Roscoe, Stella, and Travone

Clues

1. King Herod Agrippa was done by sixth grade mentor Tahoma, but not by first grade mentees Bella, Cynthia, Humphrey, or Lief.
2. Pages 6, 10, and 18 were done by first grade mentees Angel, Lief, and Travone, but the pages do not feature Asa, Nebuchadnezzar, Pharaoh, or Vashti.
3. Sixth grade mentor Margaret is paired with first grade mentee Roscoe.
4. Page 12 is done by sixth grade mentor Gabby or Hasan on Cyrus or Pharaoh.
5. Consider pages 20, 22, and 24: one was on Esther, one was on Rehoboam, and one was done with first grade mentee Roscoe.
6. The page sixth grade mentor Kiki worked on came before page 12, but the page J'waun worked on came after. Also, they did not do the page on King Saul.
7. The sixth-grade mentors are as follows: Adam, Freddie, Hasan, Kiki, Margaret Tahoma, and the mentors doing pages 4, 10, 12, 18, 20, and 24.
8. First grade mentee Lief did page 10 and his sixth-grade mentor was Freddie, Pearl, or Vladimir.
9. Consider Adam, Barry, and Freddie: their first-grade mentees are Drake, June, and Stella. Also, they are doing page numbers 2, 14, and 20.
10. First grade mentees Bella, Cynthia, June, Lief, and Travone are doing pages before page 12.
11. Sixth grade mentors Adam, Chris, and Hasan are not doing pages 4, 8, or 14.
12. The kings and queens are as follows: Ahab, Esther, Herod Agrippa, Nebuchadnezzar, Queen of Sheba, Solomon, Vashti, and the ones done by sixth grade mentors Barry, Chris, Gabby, Pearl, and Vladimir.
13. First grade mentees Bella, Drake and Ming are doing pages 4, 12, and 20.
14. Cyrus is being done by first grade mentee Angel and the Queen of Sheba is being done first grade mentee Cynthia.
15. Herod Agrippa and Vashti are pages 14 and 16.
16. Page 6 was about Solomon and page 24 was about Esther.
17. Sixth grade mentor Vladimir is not paired with first grade mentees Angel or Bella.
18. Ahab is done by sixth grade mentor Margaret.

Grid for Kings and Queens

	2	4	6	8	10	12	14	16	18	20	22	24	Angel	Bella	Cynthia	Drake	Humphrey	Joseph	June	Lief	Ming	Roscoe	Stella	Travone	Adam	Barry	Chris	Freddie	Gabby	Hasan	J'waun	Kiki	Margaret	Pearl	Tahoma	Vladimir
Ahab																																				
Asa																																				
Cyrus																																				
Esther																																				
Herod Agrippa																																				
Nebuchnezzar																																				
Pharaoh																																				
Queen of Sheba																																				
Rehoboam																																				
Saul																																				
Solomon																																				
Vashti																																				
Adam																																				
Barry																																				
Chris																																				
Freddie																																				
Gabby																																				
Hasan																																				
J'waun																																				
Kiki																																				
Margaret																																				
Pearl																																				
Tahoma																																				
Vladimir																																				
Angel																																				
Bella																																				
Cynthia																																				
Drake																																				
Humphrey																																				
Joseph																																				
June																																				
Lief																																				
Ming																																				
Roscoe																																				
Stella																																				
Travone																																				

Christian Roots

Recommended verses: See appendix
Difficulty: medium

Many companies have roots in Christianity. Some started out as organizations based on Christian principles. Some had Christian founders. Having Christian roots does not mean that all of the workers are Christian or that the people who support these organizations are Christian. These companies might lose their Christian roots over time. Having Christian roots simply means that these companies were previously influenced by Christianity.

I do not own or represent these companies. I do not claim to know their values or polices.

Categories

Name: Andrés, Brin, Christopher, Daichi, Elba, Hildegarde, Ivette, Joy, Krysanthe, Lee, Marshal, Oprah, Pablo, Stephanie, Tabitha, Victor, Wendell, and Yara

Company: Bethel University, Chick-Fil-A, Divine Image Cosmetics, eHarmony, Fellowship Travel International, Forever 21, George Foreman, Habitat for Humanity, Harvard, Hobby Lobby, In-N-Out Burger, Interstate Batteries, Lord's Gym, ServiceMaster, Thrivent Financial, Tyson Foods, Whole Foods, and YMCA

Clues

1. The companies are as follows: Bethel University, Divine Image Cosmetics, eHarmony, Forever 21, George Foreman, Habitat for Humanity, Harvard, Hobby Lobby, Interstate Batteries, Lord's Gym, ServiceMaster, Thrivent Financial, Tyson Foods, Whole Foods, and the companies being researched by Christopher, Elba, Marshal, and Victor.
2. Brin researches Harvard, Lord's Gym, or YMCA.
3. Daichi researches George Foreman, Hobby Lobby, or Lord's Gym.
4. Stephanie researches Chick-Fil-A, E Harmony, or In-N-Out Burger.
5. Krysanthe researches Bethel University, and Pablo researches Tyson Foods.
6. Consider Ivette, Oprah, and Victor: they are researching Forever 21, In-N-Out Burger, and Interstate Batteries.
7. Consider Andrés, Lee, and Tabitha: they are researching Habitat for Humanity, Lord's Gym, and Whole Foods.
8. Consider Brin, Elba, and Wendell: they are researching Fellowship Travel International, Harvard, and Thrivent Financial.
9. George Foreman is researched by Christopher or Joy.
10. Whole Foods is not researched by Tabitha, and the YMCA is not researched by Marshal.
11. Consider Andrés, Oprah, Tabitha: they are researching Habitat for Humanity, Interstate Batteries, and Whole Foods.
12. Yara is not researching Divine Image Cosmetics.

Grid for Christian Roots

	Bethel University	Chick-Fil-A	Divine Image Cosmetics	E Harmony	Fellowship Travel International	Forever 21	George Foreman	Habitat for Humanity	Harvard	Hobby Lobby	In-N-Out Burger	Interstate Batteries	Lord's Gym	ServiceMaster	Thrivent Financial	Tyson Foods	Whole Foods	YMCA
Andrés																		
Brin																		
Christopher																		
Daichi																		
Elba																		
Hildegarde																		
Ivette																		
Joy																		
Krysanthe																		
Lee																		
Marshal																		
Oprah																		
Pablo																		
Stephanie																		
Tabitha																		
Victor																		
Wendell																		
Yara																		

Christian Scientists Born Before 1700

Recommended verses: See appendix
Difficulty: easy

Throughout the years, many scientists have explored the relationship between Christianity and science. Christianity and science often have points of agreement, yet they also have their differences.

There is a course about Christian scientists (or Christians who impacted science) at the local community college. Grades are given three times a semester as part of the grading system. For the first grade, the students must write a paper on a scientist from before the 1700s. Here are their options:[38]

1. **Anton Maria of Rheita.** An astronomer who wondered if beings on other planets were cursed by original sin too.
2. **Blaise Pascal.** He is known for Pascal's law (physics), Pascal's theorem (math), and Pascal's wager (theology.)
3. **Francis Bacon.** Considered a father of empiricism; he established the scientific method used today.
4. **Isaac Barrow.** A mathematician, scientist, and theologian who wrote variety of works about the Lord's Prayer and sacraments as well as *Lectiones Opticae et Geometricae*.
5. **Isaac Newton.** An alchemist, Christian apologist, and physicist who lived during the scientific revolution. He discovered the laws of gravity.
6. **Nicholas of Cusa.** A Catholic cardinal and theologian who developed concepts of infinitesimal and relative motion.
7. **Nicole Oresme.** A theologian and former bishop of Lisieux. He is mainly known for his studies in astrogeology and mathematics.
8. **Pierre Gassendi.** A Catholic priest who investigated the relationship between atomism and Christianity. He also published works on the transit of Mercury and corrected coordinates of the Mediterranean Sea.
9. **Robert Boyle.** A Christian apologist, scientist, and theologian who believed that science glorified God. He is best known for his contributions to chemistry.
10. **William Turner.** An ornithologist and the father of English botany. He was arrested for preaching favorably about the Reformation. He became the dean of Wells Cathedral, but was expelled for nonconformity.

Match the scientist's name with the number of students who wrote about that scientist.

Categories

Scientist's name: Anton Maria of Rheita, Blaise Pascal, Francis Bacon, Isaac Barrow, Isaac Newton, Nicholas of Cusa, Nicole Oresme, Pierre Gassendi, Robert Boyle, and William Turner
Number of students who wrote about a scientist (each number appears twice): 4, 5, 6, 7, and 8

---

[38] "List of Christians in science and technology." Wikipedia. 2016. Accessed July 31, 2016. https://en.wikipedia.org/wiki/List_of_Christians_in_science_and_technology. "List of Christians in Science and Technology." *Wikipedia*. Wikimedia Foundation. Web. 31 July 2016.

Clues

1. Consider the reports on Nicole Oresme and William Turner: the number of students who wrote reports on them was 4 and 6.
2. Fewer students wrote about Pierre Gassendi than Blaise Pascal.
3. 7 or 8 students wrote about Isaac Newton, 6 or 7 students wrote about Nicholas of Cusa, 5 or 6 students wrote about Nicole Oresme, and 4 or 5 students wrote about Anton Maria of Rheita.
4. More than 6 students wrote about Robert Boyle, but fewer than 6 students wrote about Francis Bacon.
5. William Turner had the same number of people write about him as Anton Maria of Rheita or Nicholas of Cusa.
6. The same number of students wrote about Blaise Pascal and Isaac Newton.
7. More students wrote about Isaac Barrow than Isaac Newton.

Grid for Christian Scientists Born Before 1700

	4	4	5	5	6	6	7	7	8	8
Anton Maria of Rheita										
Blaise Pascal										
Francis Bacon										
Isaac Barrow										
Isaac Newton										
Nicholas of Cusa										
Nicole Oresme										
Pierre Gassendi										
Robert Boyle										
William Turner										

Christian Scientists Born 1700–1900

Recommended verses: See appendix
Difficulty: easy

Throughout the years, many scientists have explored the relationship between Christianity and science. Christianity and science often have points of agreement, yet they also have their differences.

There is a course about Christian scientists (or Christians who impacted science) at the local community college. Grades are given three times a semester as part of the grading system. For the second grade, students were sorted into five different groups, where they presented on two different scientists. These were their scientists:[39]

1. **Albrecht von Haller.** An anatomist, Christian apologist, and the father of modern physiology. He helped create the Reformed church in Göttingen and was interested in religious questions.
2. **Antoine Lavoisier.** Known as the father of modern chemistry. He is attributed with creating an early version of the periodic table of elements and the law of conservation of mass.
3. **Charles Doolittle Walcott.** A paleontologist famous for his discovery of the Burgess shale fossils of British Columbia. He believed that God planned for natural selection.
4. **Charles Glover Barkla.** A physicist who won the 1917 Nobel Prize in Physics. He studied the science involved in X-rays. He considered his work a quest for God.
5. **James David Forbes.** A physicist and glaciologist known for his studies about heat and seismology. His faith is seen in the *Life and Letters of James David Forbes*.
6. **Johannes Reinke.** A phycologist and naturalist. He founded the German Botanical Society and opposed Darwinism. He wrote *Kritik der Abstammungslehre* (*Critique of the Theory of Evolution*) and *Naturwissenschaft, Weltanschauung, Religion* (*Science, Philosophy, Religion*).
7. **John Bachman.** A scientist who named several species of animals. He wrote many scientific articles as well as articles about Lutheranism. He founded the Lutheran Theological Southern Seminary.
8. **George Washington Carver.** A botanist, educator, inventor and an activist for racial harmony. Carver felt that a belief in God was essential to understanding science.
9. **Marshall Hall.** An abolitionist and physiologist. His studies about the human body advanced medical science. He opposed slavery, calling it a sin against God. His widow created his biography, *The Memoirs of Marshall Hall*.
10. **Mary Anning.** A fossil collector and paleontologist. She discovered numerous fossils in her lifetime. Anning was devoutly religious and raised as a Dissenter (a Protestant who left the Church of England).

Match the group with the two scientists they presented on.

Categories

Group: A, B, C, D, and E
First scientist presented: Albrecht von Haller, Charles Glover Barkla, George Washington Carver, John Bachman, and Marshall Hall

---

[39] Same as #38

Second scientist presented: Antoine Lavoisier, Charles Doolittle Walcott, James David Forbes, Johannes Reinke, and Mary Anning

Clues

1. The group that first presented on George Washington Carver did not present on Charles Doolittle Walcott.
2. Albrecht von Haller was not presented by group A or E, Johannes Reinke was not presented by group C or D, John Bachman was not presented by group B or D, Marshall Hall was not presented by group C or E, and Mary Anning was not presented by group A or B.
3. Group E did its second presentation on Antoine Lavoisier.
4. Consider James David Forbes and John Bachman: one was presented by group A, and the other was presented by group C.
5. George Washington Carver was the first scientist presented by group D.
6. Group A presented on Marshall Hall.

Grid for Christian Scientists Born 1700–1900

	Albrecht von Haller	Charles Glover Barkla	George Washington Carver	John Bachman	Marshall Hall	Antoine Lavoisier	Charles Doolittle Walcott	James David Forbes	Johannes Reinke	Mary Anning
Group A										
Group B										
Group C										
Group D										
Group E										
Antoine Lavoisier										
Charles Doolittle Walcott										
James David Forbes										
Johannes Reinke										
Mary Anning										

Christian Scientists Born in the 1900s

Recommended verses: See appendix
Difficulty: hard

Throughout the years, many scientists have explored the relationship between Christianity and science. Christianity and science often have points of agreement, yet they also have their differences.

There is a course about Christian scientists (or Christians who impacted science) at the local community college. Grades are given three times a semester as part of the grading system. For the third grade, the students are divided into teams, where they must answer questions correctly to receive points.

The answers are about the following scientists:[40]

1. **C. F. von Weizsäcker**. A nuclear engineer and physicist who helped discover the Bethe-Weizsäcker formula. He wrote about the relationship between Christianity and science in his book, *The Relevance of Science: Creation and Cosmogony.*

2. **Charles H. Townes**. An inventor and physicist who won the 1964 Nobel Prize in Physics. He later wrote *The Convergence of Science and Religion*. Also, he invented the maser and the laser.

3. **George R. Price.** A chemist who converted from atheism to Christianity. He was distressed by the homeless. His scientific contributions include the Price equation and attempts to apply game theory to evolutionary biology.

4. **Jérôme Lejeune.** A geneticist who was interested in chromosome abnormalities especially regarding Down syndrome. He was part of the Pontifical Academy of Sciences and became acquainted with Pope John Paul II.

5. **Joseph Murray.** A surgeon who revolutionized transplant surgery by doing the first successful kidney transplant. In 1990, he was awarded the Nobel Prize in Physiology or Medicine.

6. **Kathleen Lonsdale.** A crystallographer who also studied diamonds. She was the first woman president of the International Union of Crystallography and the British Association for the Advancement of Science. She identified herself as a Quaker and a Christian pacifist.

7. **Mary Celine Fasenmyer.** One of the Sisters of Mercy who discovered the mathematical concept of Sister Celine's polynomials. Part of her work contributed to the creation of the WZ theory.

8. **Sir Robert Boyd.** He was an astronomer, physicist, and educator. Boyd was elected vice president of the Royal Astronomical Society. He later founded the Research Scientists' Christian Fellowship.

9. **Stanley Jaki.** A Benedictine priest, physicist, and educator. He won a Templeton Prize for his knowledge of both religion and science. Jaki believed that modern science could only have arisen in a Christian society. He was known for his ability as a lecturer.

10. **Wernher von Braun.** A well-known aerospace engineer and space architect. He developed both rockets and missiles. Braun also worked toward putting people on Mars. Despite a shady history with the Nazi party, later in life, he converted to Christianity, and this began to reshape his perceptions of science.

---

[40] Same as #38

Below are the results of two of the teams. Match the team name with the answer to the question, the name of the student who answered the question, the points each question is worth, and whether the student got the question correct or incorrect.

Categories

Team name (5 in each): Greek Scholars and Theo-tists
Answer: C. F. von Weizsäcker, Charles H. Townes, George R. Price, Jérôme Lejeune, Joseph Murray, Kathleen Lonsdale, Mary Celine Fasenmyer, Sir Robert Boyd, Stanley Jaki, and Wernher von Braun
Student name: Aurora, Buzz, Conan, Elenore, Fabian, Hazel, Kalifa, Monty, Penny, and Travis
Points each question is worth (2 of each): 100, 200, 300, 400, and 500
Correct or incorrect (5 of each): correct and incorrect

Clues

1. The Greek Scholars got three questions correct.
2. The question with the answer "Mary Celine Fasenmyer" was answered incorrectly.
3. Both of the 500-point questions were answered correctly.
4. The members of the Theo-tists are as follows: Conan, Elenore, Monty, and the people who answered the questions about George R. Price and Sir Robert Boyd.
5. The questions answered incorrectly are worth 100, 200, 200, 300, and 400 points.
6. The students who answered their questions correctly are Conan, Hazel, Kalifa, Penny, and Travis.
7. Fabian's question was about Joseph Murray or Mary Celine Fasenmyer.
8. Monty's question was about George R. Price or Jérôme Lejeune.
9. Aurora's question was about George R. Price or Kathleen Lonsdale.
10. The answers "C. F. von Weizsäcker" and "Kathleen Lonsdale" are both worth 100 points.
11. Penny is not on the same team as Buzz, and Conan is not on the same team as Hazel.
12. Someone on the Greek Scholars answered the question about Stanley Jaki.
13. The person who answered the question about C. F. von Weizsäcker was Aurora, Elenore, or Fabian.
14. Consider Buzz, Monty, and Travis: The questions they answered were worth 200, 300, and 400 points.
15. Kalifa, who is on the Greek Scholars team, answered a 500-point question.
16. The 400-point questions are about Charles H. Townes and Wernher von Braun, and these questions are answered by Buzz and Conan.
17. Aurora is a Theo-ist.
18. The question about Mary Celine Fasenmyer is worth 300 points, but is not answered by Buzz or Travis, and the Joseph Murray question is not worth 500 points.
19. The question about Charles H. Townes is answered by a Greek Scholar.

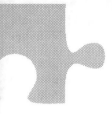

Grid for Christian Scientists Born in the 1900s

	C. F. von Weizsäcker	Charles H. Townes	George R. Price	Jérôme Lejeune	Joseph Murray	Kathleen Lonsdale	Mary Celine Fasenmyer	Sir Robert Boyd	Stanley Jaki	Wernher von Braun	Correct	Incorrect	100	200	300	400	500	Aurora	Buzz	Conan	Elenore	Fabian	Hazel	Kalifa	Monty	Penny	Travis
Greek Scholars																											
Greek Scholars																											
Greek Scholars																											
Greek Scholars																											
Greek Scholars																											
Theo-tists																											
Theo-tists																											
Theo-tists																											
Theo-tists																											
Theo-tists																											
Aurora																											
Buzz																											
Conan																											
Elenore																											
Fabian																											
Hazel																											
Kalifa																											
Monty																											
Penny																											
Travis																											
100																											
100																											
200																											
200																											
300																											
300																											
400																											
400																											
500																											
500																											
Correct																											
Incorrect																											

Prophets and Prophetesses Vol. 1

Recommended verses: See appendix

Difficulty: easy

Prophets and prophetesses are people who bring messages from God to specific people and nations. They often bring news about future events, indicating what will happen. Prophets and prophetesses do not always bring bad news; they simply bring the news from God. When a prophet brings bad news, repentance from the offender can sometimes change God's mind and avert disaster. An example of this is Jonah 3:1–10. In addition, some prophets have their own books in the Bible. These books tend to be very short; some are less than four chapters long.

It should also be noted that the Bible warns about false prophets. Their messages often contradict the rulings of God the Father and the teachings of Jesus.

Here is a bit of information about a few prophets and prophetesses:

1. **Deborah.** A wise woman, prophetess, and wife. She was one of the judges of Israel responsible for fighting against idolatry in the land. Deborah sent for Barak to join her in war against the Canaanites.

2. **Habakkuk.** A minor prophet about whom little personal information is known. He delivered five prophetic messages and one song of praise to God. He also wrote the book of Habakkuk.

3. **Hosea.** A prophet who God told to marry a promiscuous woman to parallel the relationship between God and Israel. Gomer had at least three children, and at least one of them was not Hosea's. Gomer ran off with a lover and ended up in slavery, but Hosea bought her back.

4. **Lucius of Cyrene.** A prophet, Jew, part of the Christian church in Antioch, and the first bishop of Cyrene. He likely prayed and fasted before sending Barnabas and Paul (formerly Saul) off to do missionary work. He is mentioned very little in the Bible.

5. **Miriam.** Sister of Aaron and Moses and a prophetess. She watched baby Moses on the Nile and spent many years as a slave in Egypt. Miriam briefly suffered from leprosy after she challenged Moses's leadership.

6. **Nahum.** A minor prophet who warned the city of Nineveh of its impending destruction. He wrote the book of Nahum and lived among the Elkoshites.

7. **Obadiah.**[41] A prophet and Edomite who was chosen to prophesize to Edom. Supposedly, he is same Obadiah who hid hundreds of God's prophets from King Ahab and Queen Jezebel. It was said that he was rewarded with the gift of prophecy.

8. **Philip the Evangelist.** God sent him down a road, where he met an Ethiopian, who served the Ethiopian queen. Philip helped the man understand a scripture about Jesus, and the man was baptized. Philip spent time in Samaria talking about Jesus and removing demons from people.

Match the name of the person with the prophet or prophetess he or she is learning about.

Categories

Name: Akito, Evan, Hernán, Jade, Nakita, Shanice, Tobias, and Yasmina

Prophets and Prophetesses: Deborah, Habakkuk, Hosea, Lucius of Cyrene, Miriam, Nahum, Obadiah and Philip the Evangelist

---

[41] "Obadiah." *Wikipedia*. Wikimedia Foundation. Web. 02 Aug. 2016.

Clues

1. Consider Akito, Shanice, and Yasmina: they are interested in Lucius of Cyrene, Miriam, and Obadiah.
2. Philip the Evangelist is being researched by Evan or Tobias.
3. Deborah is being researched Hernán or Nakita.
4. If Akito is interested in Lucius of Cyrene, then Jade is interested in Habakkuk.
5. Evan, Hernán, and Shanice are not interested in Hosea or Obadiah.
6. Jade, Tobias, and Yasmina are interested in Habakkuk, Miriam, and Nahum.

Grid for Prophets and Prophetesses Vol. 1

	Deborah	Habakkuk	Hosea	Lucius of Cyrene	Miriam	Nahum	Obadiah	Philip the Evangelist
Akito								
Evan								
Hernán								
Jade								
Nakita								
Shanice								
Tobias								
Yasmina								

Prophets and Prophetesses Vol. 2

Recommended verses: See appendix

Difficulty: easy

Prophets and prophetesses are people who bring messages from God to specific people and nations. They often bring news about future events, indicating what will happen. Prophets and prophetesses do not always bring bad news; they simply bring the news from God. When a prophet brings bad news, repentance from the offender can sometimes change God's mind and avert disaster. An example of this is Jonah 3:1–10. In addition, some prophets have their own books in the Bible. These books tend to be very short; some are less than four chapters long.

It should also be noted that the Bible warns about false prophets. Their messages often contradict the rulings of God the Father and the teachings of Jesus.

Here is a bit of information about a few prophets and prophetesses:

1. **Anna.** A prophetess who never left the temple but continually fasted, prayed, and worshiped God. When she saw the baby Jesus, she prophesized about how he would redeem Jerusalem.
2. **The apostle Paul (formerly called Saul).** He killed followers of Jesus, until God blinded him. Ananias healed his sight, and then Paul traveled across Eurasia preaching about Jesus. Paul started many churches before his final imprisonment and death. He wrote at least eight books of the New Testament, possibly thirteen.
3. **The four daughters of Philip the Evangelist.** Mentioned in only one verse of the Bible, these unnamed, single virgins who prophesized.[42] They were likely fully-grown women.
4. **Elijah.** The prophet who went up against King Ahab, Queen Jezebel, and their worship of the false god Baal.
5. **Haggai.** He was the first prophet since the Babylonia exile. Haggai declared that it was time to finish rebuilding the temple.
6. **John the Baptist.** His mother Elizabeth was a cousin of Jesus's mother, Mary. John's main prophetic message was that the messiah (Jesus) was coming. Baptism was an important part of his ministry. He baptized Jesus. John was imprisoned and beheaded by King Herod.
7. **Moses.** This prophet was born a Hebrew slave and set adrift in a basket, only to be taken in by the daughter of the pharaoh. He committed murder and fled for his life, only to return years later after speaking with God through a burning bush. He led the Hebrews out of Egypt and guided them for many years in the desert.
8. **Zephaniah.** A son of Cushi and a descendent of King Hezekiah, he prophesized about the upcoming judgment on Judah, Jerusalem, the nation of Israel's enemies, and a few other nations. He is also attributed with a song of praise to God.

Categories

Name: Bob, Daffodil, Fumiko, Gregory, Hironobu, Marina, Octavia, and Wendy

Prophets and Prophetesses: Anna, the apostle Paul, the four daughters of Philip the Evangelist, Elijah, Haggai, John the Baptist, Moses, and Zephaniah

---

[42] "Acts 21 NIV." Bible Hub, 1973–2011. Web. 2 Aug. 2016.

Clues

1. Daffodil researches the apostle Paul or John the Baptist.
2. Bob and Fumiko do not research Anna or Moses.
3. Gregory and Marina do not research Elijah or the four daughters of Philip the Evangelist.
4. Zephaniah is researched by Bob or Octavia.
5. If Fumiko researches John the Baptist, then Hironobu researches Moses.
6. If Marina researches the apostle Paul, then Gregory researches Haggai.
7. The prophets and prophetesses are as follows: the apostle Paul, the four daughters of Philip the Evangelist, Elijah, and Haggai, and the prophets and prophetesses researched by Bob, Daffodil, Hironobu, and Wendy.
8. Marina does not research Haggai, and Octavia does not research Elijah.
9. Fumiko researches Elijah.

Grid for Prophets and Prophetesses Vol. 2

	Anna	The Apostle Paul	Four daughters of Philip the Evangelist	Elijah	Haggai	John the Baptist	Moses	Zephaniah
Bob								
Daffodil								
Fumiko								
Gregory								
Hironobu								
Marina								
Octavia								
Wendy								

God Used Them

Recommended verses: See appendix
Difficulty: hard

Have you ever heard someone say "God can't use me?" What was that person's excuse? Usually, people say they are too young, too old, too busy, too dumb, too dishonest, and so on. The truth of the matter is that God can use anybody at any time and in any place. There are no restrictions on whom God can use. Here are some examples from the Bible:

1. **Balaam's donkey.** This donkey saved Balaam's life a few times and indirectly influenced the fate of the Israelites (Balaam almost cursed the Israelites, but he blessed them instead.) Moreover, God made this donkey speak to Balaam.
2. **Blind man.** Jesus often healed the blind. Moreover, the people who saw these healings believed in Jesus. Later on, God used blindness to change Saul into Paul.
3. **Demon-possessed man.** There are many stories of Jesus removing demons from people. The removal of the demon(s) allowed the person to have a normal life, but it also allowed many people to believe in God.
4. **Jacob.** He was liar, a cheater, and a trickster. God changed his name to Israel and used him to father the twelve tribes of Israel. His son Joseph saved everybody from starving to death during seven years of famine. Jesus was a distant descendent of his son Judah.
5. **John the Baptist.** God used him both as an unborn child and as a man. John's birth was miraculous, and the unborn John leapt inside of his mother, Elizabeth, prompting her to prophesize about Mary's baby, Jesus. John too prophesized about Jesus's arrival, and his ministry highlighted the importance of baptism.
6. **Lazarus.** He was dead. Yes, Jesus used a dead man to teach people about the power of God. Lazarus was brought back to life after three days, and many people believed in God.
7. **Leah.** The wife of Jacob. She had "tender eyes" and may or may not have been ugly, but was definitely unloved, even hated. God makes her the mother of six of the twelve tribes of Israel (more than any other woman.) Jesus was born through a descendent of her son Judah.
8. **Moses.** He was a stuttering murderer with an identity crisis. He was born a Hebrew and raised in the household of the Egyptian pharaoh, who had originally tried to kill him as a baby. He killed an Egyptian, fled into desert, and was recruited by God in the wilderness to free the Israelites from slavery.
9. **Naaman's wife's servant.** She was a slave girl and a child. She had no reason to help her master, who was the army commander for the king of Aram. Still, she told him about the prophet Elisha. As a result, Naaman was healed and promised to make sacrifices only to God.
10. **Noah.** He was a drunk. God had Noah build an ark and load up two of every animal and his family onto it. Then God flooded the world for forty days. Everybody on the ark was relieved to finally get off. Unfortunately, Noah celebrated a little too hard with the wine.
11. **Peter.** He was a fearful failure. When Peter saw Jesus walking on the water, he tried to walk on water too. Peter got spooked and started to drown. Later, Peter vowed to never abandon Jesus, but then denied knowing him when Jesus was about to be crucified. Peter eventually spread the news about Jesus across Eurasia.
12. **Rahab.** She was a prostitute who risked her life to save some Israelite spies. She persuaded the spies to spare her and her household. She gave birth to Boaz, whose descendant was Jesus.

13. **Samaritan Woman.** She was an outcast on the edge of society who married five times. She had a conversation with Jesus about living water. Many Samaritans believed in Jesus because of her testimony.

14. **Samuel.** He was a child raised away from parents. He worked under Eli, the temple priest. God called to Samuel in the night, but Samuel did not even recognize God's voice. Samuel lived a long life as God's prophet. He prepared both Saul and David for kingship.

15. **Sarah.** She was an old, barren woman who laughed at God. God promised that a nation would come through Abraham and, later on, announced that Sarah would become pregnant. Sarah laughed at this idea and was caught. Still, she gave birth to Isaac. Abraham and Sarah are the first confirmed people in Jesus's lineage.

16. **Saul.** He was the first king of Israel. He tried to kill David out of fear that David would take his throne. After consulting a witch, the ghost of the prophet Samuel revealed that Saul would die in battle the next day. During the brief period when Saul obeyed God, he had many military victories.

Students are presenting on people God used to accomplish his goals. They present on someone from the Old Testament and the New Testament, and receive one averaged grade for the two presentations. Match the name of the student with the Old and New Testament person he or she presented on and the grade he or she averaged.

Categories

Name: Anika, Emilio, Herman, Kyla, Lance, Maylene, Phineas, and Whitney
Old Testament people: Jacob, Leah, Moses, Noah, Rahab, Samuel, Sarah, and Saul
New Testament people: Balaam's donkey, blind man, demon-possessed man, John the Baptist, Lazarus, Naaman's wife's servant, Peter, and the Samaritan woman
Grade: A, A-, B+, B, B-, C+, C, and C-

Clues

1. Naaman's wife's servant was not done by Emilio or the person who presented on Sarah.
2. The grade Herman earned was higher than the grade earned by the person who presented on Samuel.
3. Anika, Herman, Lance, and Phineas did not present on Leah or Noah.
4. Consider Anika, Kyla, and Phineas: one did the presentation on Balaam's donkey, one did the presentation on the blind man, and one person averaged a B-.
5. The students who presented are as follows: Kyla; Phineas; the ones who presented on Leah, Noah, and Rahab from the Old Testament; the one who presented on Lazarus from the New Testament; and the ones who averaged a B+ and a C-.
6. The demon-possessed man was presented by Kyla or Whitney.
7. The person who presented on Rahab also presented on Peter.
8. The person who presented on Noah also presented on the demon-possessed man or John the Baptist.
9. The person who presented on Balaam's donkey averaged a B.
10. Whitney's grade is higher than Lance's, but lower than Anika's.
11. The A and A- were earned by the people who presented on Moses and Rahab.
12. Anika did not present on Balaam's donkey, Maylene did not present on Naaman's wife's servant, and Whitney did not present on John the Baptist.

13. The B+, B, and B- were averaged by the people who presented on Samuel, Sarah, and Saul.

14. Herman averaged an A-, Kyla averaged a B, and Whitney averaged a C.

15. The person who presented on Noah also presented on the demon-possessed man.

16. The person who presented on Leah was Herman or Maylene.

17. The person presenting on Sarah received a lower average than the person presenting on Samuel.

18. Naaman's wife's servant earned a B-, but was not presented by the same person who presented on Sarah.

Grid for God Used Them

	Jacob	Leah	Moses	Noah	Rahab	Samuel	Sarah	Saul	A	A-	B+	B	B-	C+	C	C-	Balaam's Donkey	Blind Man	Demon Possessed Man	John the Baptist	Lazarus	Naaman's wife's servant	Peter	Samaritan woman
Anika																								
Emilio																								
Herman																								
Kyla																								
Lance																								
Maylene																								
Phineas																								
Whitney																								
Balaam's Donkey																								
Blind Man																								
Demon Possessed Man																								
John the Baptist																								
Lazarus																								
Naaman's wife's servant																								
Peter																								
Samaritan woman																								
A																								
A-																								
B+																								
B																								
B-																								
C+																								
C																								
C-																								

God Can Use You Too

Recommended verses: See appendix
Difficulty: hard

In the Bible, God used many different people to do great things in his name. Today, God can still use anybody. No label is stronger than God, including age, race, gender, income, occupation, beliefs, or intelligence.

The following people are each stuck with a label that society has given them. Despite the labels, God works through each person during one day this week. Match the name of the person with the label society has given him or her and the day of the week that God works through that person.

Categories

Name: Anton, Clay, Devin, Ginevra, Heidi, Jackie, Kyoto, Laqueta, Maebelle, Otis, Paul, Rin, Saddie, Sherece, Theo, and Uri

Label: alcoholic, atheist, celebrity, college graduate, dying, fourth grade education, healthy, introvert, janitor, married, newborn, Parkinson's disease, prisoner, unemployed, wealthy, and wheelchair bound

Day (Sunday and Monday occur three times, all other days occur two times): Sunday, Monday, Tuesday, Wednesday, Thursday, Friday, and Saturday

Clue

1. Clay's label is not "fourth grade education," Heidi is not wealthy, Laqueta is not an introvert, Paul is not an atheist, and Uri is not unemployed.
2. Saddie sees God in her life on Saturday or Sunday.
3. The people who see God in their lives on Tuesday are the person with Parkinson's disease and Anton.
4. The person who is an alcoholic saw God in his or her life on Monday.
5. Consider the people who saw God in their lives on Sunday: one is dying, one has a fourth-grade education, and one is married.
6. Ginevra is healthy, but she did not see God in her life on the same day as Kyoto or Rin.
7. Consider the people who saw God in their lives on Wednesday: they are Clay and Devin. Also, one of them is a janitor, and one is an atheist.
8. Maebelle is a celebrity, but she did not see God in her life on Monday or Thursday.
9. The person who is wealthy and Rin saw God in their lives on the same day of the week, which was Thursday or Friday.
10. The prisoner, who saw God in his life on Saturday, was Anton or Paul.
11. Consider Devin, Otis, and Saddie: one is an atheist, one is a college graduate, and one had a fourth-grade education.
12. Paul and Maebelle see God in their lives on the same day of the week.
13. Consider Anton, Jackie, and Theo: one is an alcoholic, one is a newborn, and one is unemployed.
14. The college graduate saw God in his or her life on Monday, Kyoto saw God in his life on Tuesday, and Laqueta saw God in her life on Friday.
15. Theo saw God in his life the day before Rin did, and Sherece saw God in her life two days before Kyoto did.
16. Consider Heidi, Laqueta, and Uri: one is dying, one is wealthy, and one is wheelchair bound.
17. If Anton is the newborn, then he must have seen God in his life on Thursday.
18. Uri is dying, and the wheelchair-bound person did not see God in his or her life on Monday.

Grid for God Can Use You Too

	Alcoholic	Atheist	Celebrity	College Graduate	Dying	Fourth Grade Education	Healthy	Introvert	Janitor	Married	Newborn	Parkinson's Disease	Prisoner	Unemployed	Wealthy	Wheelchair Bound	Sunday	Sunday	Sunday	Monday	Monday	Monday	Tuesday	Tuesday	Wednesday	Wednesday	Thursday	Thursday	Friday	Friday	Saturday	Saturday
Anton																																
Clay																																
Devin																																
Ginevra																																
Heidi																																
Jackie																																
Kyoto																																
Laqueta																																
Maebelle																																
Otis																																
Paul																																
Rin																																
Saddie																																
Sherece																																
Theo																																
Uri																																
Sunday																																
Sunday																																
Sunday																																
Monday																																
Monday																																
Monday																																
Tuesday																																
Tuesday																																
Wednesday																																
Wednesday																																
Thursday																																
Thursday																																
Friday																																
Friday																																
Saturday																																
Saturday																																

Family Day at the Zoo

Recommended verses: See appendix
Difficulty: hard

These Christian families are enjoying a day at the zoo. They get to see animals that God created that they normally do not see. Can you match the family name with the family's favorite animal, the food the family ate, and the number of family members?

Categories

Family: Abrams, Elder, Hamilton, Jurgensen, Lenoir, Marsh, Ortberg, Quigg, Reeves, Sanders, Tally, and Yanos

Animal: African elephant, flamingo, Galápagos tortoise, giraffe, gorilla, koala, lion, penguin, polar bear, sea lion, snow leopard, and tiger

Food: burger, chicken nuggets, corn cob, cotton candy, grilled cheese, hot dog, ice cream, pizza, popcorn, pretzel, salad, and snow cone

Number of family members: 1, 2, 3 (occurs two times), 4 (occurs three times), 5 (occurs three times), 6, and 7

Clues

1. The family that favored the snow leopard was the Elder, Marsh, or Reeves family.
2. The families with four members each did not the favor the flamingo, lion, or tiger.
3. Snow cones are eaten by the family that favored the flamingos, which was the Abrams, Marsh, Quigg, or Tally family.
4. The family that favored the polar bear had two more members than the family that favored the snow leopard.
5. The family with one member does not favor the flamingo and did not eat pizza.
6. Consider the families with 1, 2, and 7 members: one is the Abrams family, one family favors the penguin, and one family eats salad.
7. The Tally family and the family that favors the giraffes has the same number of family members.
8. The Hamilton family ate ice cream, the Ortberg family ate cotton candy, and the family that favored the Galápagos tortoise ate salad. All of them had at least 3 family members.
9. Consider the Hamilton, Jurgensen, and Lenoir families: they favor the gorilla, the koalas, and the sea lion. Also, each family has a different number of members.
10. The family that favors the penguins is Elder or Sanders.
11. The number of family members in the Elder family plus the number of family members in the Quigg family equals the number of family members in the Yanos family.
12. The snow leopard was favored by a family with four members, and so was the African elephant, but not the giraffe, koala, or sea lion.
13. The family that ate the pretzels had fewer members than the Quigg family, and the family that ate the hot dog had at least five members.
14. Consider the Sanders, Tally, and Yanos families: one favored the African elephant, one favored the flamingo, and one had seven family members.
15. Consider the families with five members: they are the Jurgensens, the family that favored the giraffe, and the family that favored the flamingo. They ate hot dogs, pizza, and snow cones.
16. The Quigg family has more than four members, but the Lenoir family has fewer than four.

17. The family that favored the sea lion ate pretzels and had 3 family members, the family that favored the lion ate grilled cheese and had 2 family members, and the Marsh family ate corn on the cob.

18. The size of the family that ate the chicken nuggets is greater than the size of the Abrams family but smaller than the size of the Reeves family.

19. The Reeves family does not eat pizza, and the family that favors the polar bear does not eat popcorn.

Grid for Family Day at the Zoo

	African Elephant	Flamingo	Galápagos Tortoise	Giraffe	Gorilla	Koala	Lion	Penguin	Polar Bear	Sea Lion	Snow Leopard	Tiger	1	2	3	3	4	4	4	5	5	5	6	7	Burger	Chicken Nuggets	Corn Cob	Cotton Candy	Grilled Cheese	Hot Dog	Ice Cream	Pizza	Popcorn	Pretzel	Salad	Snow Cone
Abrams																																				
Elder																																				
Hamilton																																				
Jurgensen																																				
Lenoir																																				
Marsh																																				
Ortberg																																				
Quigg																																				
Reeves																																				
Sanders																																				
Tally																																				
Yanos																																				
Burger																																				
Chicken Nuggets																																				
Corn Cob																																				
Cotton Candy																																				
Grilled Cheese																																				
Hot Dog																																				
Ice Cream																																				
Pizza																																				
Popcorn																																				
Pretzel																																				
Salad																																				
Snow Cone																																				
1																																				
2																																				
3																																				
3																																				
4																																				
4																																				
4																																				
5																																				
5																																				
5																																				
6																																				
7																																				

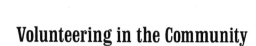

Volunteering in the Community

Recommended verses: See appendix
Difficulty: medium

Part of serving God is serving other people. Christians are called to reach out and help others, not out of obligation but out of love. Just as God gives to us every day, we are encouraged to give to others. We might even see bits of God in other people because we are all made in his image.

Match the name of the person with the place where he or she volunteers and the number of weeks he or she has volunteered.

Categories

Name: Alastair, Bellissa, Chieko, Flannery, Huey, Jonathan, Katrine, May, Niles, Pearlina, Susan, and Taj
Volunteers at: animal shelter, community center, day care, disaster relief team, high school, homeless shelter, medical clinic, middle school, museum, refugee center, retirement home, and veteran services center
Number of weeks: 2, 4, 6, 8, 10, 12, 14, 16, 18, 20, 22, and 24

Clues

1. If Bellissa has volunteered for 12 weeks, then Huey volunteers with the disaster relief team.
2. If Niles volunteers for 2 weeks, then Katrine volunteers for 20 weeks.
3. If Jonathan volunteers at the medical clinic, then May has volunteered for 22 weeks.
4. If Pearlina volunteers at the high school, then Taj volunteers at the museum.
5. If Flannery volunteers at the community center, then Jonathan volunteers at the animal shelter.
6. The people who volunteered are as follows: Bellissa, Chieko, and Katrine; the people who volunteered at the animal shelter, medical clinic, and refugee center; and the people who volunteered for 2, 4, 10, 14, 18, and 22 weeks.
7. The people who volunteered from 10 to 16 weeks are Chieko, Flannery, Pearlina, and Taj.
8. Consider Alastair, Bellissa, and Chieko: they have volunteered for 8, 16, and 24 weeks, but not at the animal shelter, homeless shelter, museum, or the veteran services center.
9. The person who volunteered at the day care was there for 14 weeks, and the person who volunteered at the retirement home was there for 8 weeks.
10. May volunteered at the veteran services center for 18 or 22 weeks, Niles volunteered at the homeless shelter for 2 or 6 weeks, and Taj volunteered at the day care for 10 or 14 weeks.
11. Consider the people who volunteered at the animal shelter, the community center, and the medical clinic: they are Alastair, Flannery, and Jonathan.
12. May has volunteered for 18 weeks, which is fewer than Katrine, but more than Susan.
13. The museum volunteer has been there for 20 weeks, and the disaster relief team volunteer has been there for 4 weeks.
14. Huey volunteers at the middle school, and Jonathan volunteers at the animal shelter, but Chieko did not volunteer at the museum.

Grid for Volunteering in the Community

	Animal Shelter	Community Center	Day Care	Diaster Relief Team	High School	Homeless Shelter	Medical Clinic	Middle School	Museum	Refugee Center	Retirement Home	Veteran Services Center	2	4	6	8	10	12	14	16	18	20	22	24
Alastair																								
Bellissa																								
Chieko																								
Flannery																								
Huey																								
Jonathan																								
Katrine																								
May																								
Niles																								
Pearlina																								
Susan																								
Taj																								
2													
4													
6													
8													
10													
12													
14													
16													
18													
20													
22													
24													

John 3:16–17

Recommended verses: See verse listed below
Difficulty: easy

There is an iconic Bible passage that summarizes a core belief of the Christian faith:

> For God so loved the world that he gave his one and only Son, that whoever believes in him shall not perish but have eternal life. For God did not send his Son into the world to condemn the world, but to save the world through him. —John 3:16–17

A group of children are learning John 3:16–17. They break the verse into five different parts. If everyone can learn one part, then they can put all of the parts together to learn the rest faster. Can you match the name of the child with the part they are memorizing?

Categories

Name: Ashley, Hasina, Jamal, Lita, and Tom
Part: 1, 2, 3, 4, and 5

Clues

1. Ashley is learning part 2 or 4.
2. Jamal is not learning part 2, 3, or 4.
3. Lita is learning part 5.
4. Tom is learning part 1 or 3.
5. Hasina is learning part 2.

Grid for John 3:16–17

	1	2	3	4	5
Ashley					
Hasina					
Jamal					
Lita					
Tom					

The Lord's Prayer

Recommended verses: Matthew 6:9–13
Difficulty: easy

> Our Father in heaven,
> may your name be kept holy.
> May your Kingdom come soon.
> May your will be done on earth,
> as it is in heaven.
> Give us today the food we need,
> and forgive us our sins,
> as we have forgiven those who sin against us.
> And don't let us yield to temptation,
> but rescue us from the evil one.
> For thine is the kingdom,
> The power, and the glory,
> For ever and ever. Amen.
>
> —Matthew 6:9–13 NIV

Jesus taught his disciples this prayer in Matthew 6:9–13. The part that reads "for thine is the kingdom …" was added at a later date. This prayer acknowledges the power and position of God while asking for physical, emotional, and spiritual protection.

To be confirmed, the confirmation student must recite the Lord's Prayer to the pastor in two weeks' time. They break the Lord's Prayer into six parts, so each person can learn it easily. The order in which they will meet the pastor has already been decided. Match the student's name with the part of the Lord's Prayer that he or she is currently learning and the order he or she will meet with the pastor.

Categories

Name: Anna-Marie, Nathan, Pedro, Rebecca, Stan, and Uma
Part: 1, 2, 3, 4, 5, and 6
Order to meet with the pastor: First, second, third, fourth, fifth, and sixth

Clues

1. Anna-Marie will meet with the pastor before Rebecca.
2. Consider Nathan and Stan: they are memorizing parts 3 and 6 of the Lord's Prayer, and they will be the fifth and sixth students to meet with the pastor.
3. Pedro is learning part 1 or 5 of the Lord's Prayer, and Uma is learning part 2 or 4 of the Lord's Prayer.
4. The third person to meet with the pastor is memorizing the part 4 of the Lord's Prayer.
5. The students are as follows: Anna-Marie, Nathan, Pedro, the student memorizing the part 2 of the Lord's Prayer, and the fourth and fifth students going to the pastor.
6. The student who is learning part 1 of the Lord's Prayer is the second person going to the pastor.
7. Anna-Marie is not the first person going to the pastor, but she is memorizing part 4.
8. The person who is memorizing part 6 is the sixth person to see the pastor.

Grid for The Lord's Prayer

	Part 1	Part 2	Part 3	Part 4	Part 5	Part 6	1st	2nd	3rd	4th	5th	6th
Anna-Marie												
Nathan												
Pedro												
Rebecca												
Stan												
Uma												
1st												
2nd												
3rd												
4th												
5th												
6th												

Reacting to Violence and Hate

Recommended verses: See verses listed below
Difficulty: easy

Sin has filled the world with brokenness, including violence and hate. Fortunately, the Bible gives us examples of how to deal with violence and hate, as well as gives us hope that things will get better. Just remember, every Bible verse has a context with a person, time, and place where the action makes sense. Altering a Bible verse to fit a certain situation will likely bring harm instead of healing. In other words, use the Bible as an example, but be aware of how your own situation is different, and pray to God when decisions need to made.

After a tragic event, a community is shaken by violence and hate. Many of the residents are overcome by hopelessness. These twelve residents have opened their Bibles. They hope to find answers in its pages; they hope that God will hear their prayers. Match the name of the resident with the verse that he or she found.

Categories

Name: Ambrose, Corbin, Dawn, Eli, Hank, Jane, Kalim, Lindsey, Payton, Rosaleen, Seanna, and Viola
Verse: Acts 17:26, Ephesians 6:10–18, Galatians 3: 28–29, James 2:1–13, James 2:14–26, Job 2:11–13, Luke 10:25–37, Luke 18:1–8, Matthew 5:23–26, Matthew 18:15–17, Psalm 11:5, and 2 Corinthians 5:18–21

Clues

1. Corbin read a verse in Matthew, Jane read a verse in James, and Payton read a verse in Luke.
2. Consider Ambrose, Eli, and Seanna: they read the verses Ephesians 6:10–18, Matthew 18:15–17, and Psalm 11:5.
3. Dawn's verse is not in James or Luke.
4. Consider Hank, Kalim, and Rosaleen: they read Galatians 3:28–29, Luke 18:1–8, and 2 Corinthians 5:18–21.
5. Seanna's verse is not Ephesians 6:10–18.
6. The people are as follows: Ambrose, Corbin, Dawn, Hank, Lindsey, and the people who read Ephesians 6:10–18, Galatians 3: 28–29, James 2:14–16, Job 2:11–13, Luke 10:25–37, Psalm 11:5, and 2 Corinthians 5:18–21.
7. Kalim did not read 2 Corinthians 5:18–21.

Grid for Reacting to Violence and Hate

	Acts 17:26	Ephesians 6:10-18	Galatians 3: 28-29	James 2:1-13	James 2:14-2:26	Job 2:11-13	Luke 10:25-37	Luke 18:1-8	Matthew 5:23-26	Matthew 18:15-17	Psalm 11:5	2 Corinthians 5:18-21
Ambrose												
Corbin												
Dawn												
Eli												
Hank												
Jane												
Kalim												
Lindsey												
Payton												
Rosaleen												
Seanna												
Viola												

My Soul Is Still Singing

Recommended verses: See appendix
Difficulty: hard

Songs are powerful. They share feelings, and they share knowledge. They tell stories, and they relay messages. If you have ever been to a church service, the odds are that you have heard at least one song. Maybe the song expressed what you wanted to say; maybe not. Church is not the only place to hear songs about God. Many artists have created modern versions of traditional church hymns, while others have created completely new songs.

The following puzzle is about ten Christians, their favorite traditional church hymns, and their favorite modern Christian songs. Use the clues to fill in the grid.

Categories

Name: Bruno, Carmen, Hakeen, Isabeau, Kelvin, Maggie, Phoebe, Quigley, Tanishia, and Zoe
Church hymn: "A Mighty Fortress Is Our God," "Amazing Grace," "Battle Hymn of the Republic," "Gather Us In," "Let There Be Peace on Earth," "Lift High the Cross," "My Hope Is Built on Nothing Less," "Psalm 141: Let My Prayer Rise Up," "The Light of That City," and "What a Friend We Have in Jesus"

Modern Christian song:

- "Be One" by Natalie Grant
- "Beyond the Moon and Stars" by Dan Schutte
- "Cry to Jesus" by Third Day
- "God Bless America" by the Gaither Vocal Band
- "Jesus Take the Wheel" by Carrie Underwood
- "Lord, I Lift Your Name on High" by Hill Song
- "Lose My Soul" by Toby Mac, featuring Franklin Kirk and Mandisa
- "Open the Eyes of My Heart" by Michael W. Smith
- "Smile/Better Is One Day in Your Courts" by Jonathan Nelson
- "Trust in You" by Lauren Daigle

Clues

1. "Trust in You" is the favorite modern Christian song of Hakeen, Maggie, or Quigley.
2. The person who favors "Gather Us In" also favors "Beyond the Moon and Stars."
3. Consider Isabeau, Maggie, and Tanishia: they favor the modern Christian songs "God Bless America," "Jesus Take the Wheel," and "Smile/Better Is One Day in Your Courts."
4. "My Hope Is Built on Nothing Less" is Zoe's favorite hymn.
5. "Amazing Grace" is favored by the same person who favors "Jesus Take the Wheel."
6. Consider Bruno, Phoebe, and Zoe: they favor the hymns "Psalm 141: Let My Prayer Rise Up" and "What a Friend We Have in Jesus" and the modern Christian song "Lose My Soul."
7. "Lord, I Lift Your Name on High" is the favorite modern Christian song of Bruno, Hakeen, or Quigley.
8. Tanisha favors "God Bless America," and Isabeau favors "Smile/Better Is One Day in Your Courts."
9. Hakeen favors "Battle Hymn of the Republic," and Quigley favors "The Light of the City."
10. "A Mighty Fortress Is Our God" is favored by the person who favors "Be One."
11. "What a Friend We Have in Jesus" is favored by the person who favors "Open the Eyes of My Heart," but this person is not Phoebe.

12. "Beyond the Moon and Stars" is not favored by Kelvin, but "Lord, I Lift Your Name on High" is favored by Hakeen.

13. "Let There Be Peace on Earth" is not favored by Isabeau.

Grid for My Soul Is Still Singing

	A Might Fortress is Our God	Amazing Grace	Battle Hymn of the Republic	Gather Us In	Let There Be Peace on Earth	Lift High the Cross	My Hope is Built on Nothing Less	Psalm 141-Let My Prayer Rise Up	The Light of That City	What a Friend We Have in Jesus	Be One by Natalie Grant	Beyond the Moon and Stars by Dan Schutte	Cry to Jesus by Third Day	God Bless America by The Gaither Vocal Band	Jesus Take the Wheel by Carrie Underwood	Lord I Lift Your Name on High by Hill Song	Lose My Soul by Toby Mac, featuring Franklin Kirk and Mandisa	Open the Eyes of My Heart by Michael W. Smith	Smile/Better is One Day in Your Courts by Jonathan Nelson	Trust In You by Lauren Daigle
Bruno																				
Carmen																				
Hakeen																				
Isabeau																				
Kelvin																				
Maggie																				
Phoebe																				
Quigley																				
Tanishia																				
Zoe																				
Be One by Natalie Grant																				
Beyond the Moon and Stars by Dan Schutte																				
Cry to Jesus by Third Day																				
God Bless America by The Gaither Vocal Band																				
Jesus Take the Wheel by Carrie Underwood																				
Lord I Lift Your Name on High by Hill Song																				
Lose My Soul by Toby Mac, featuring Franklin Kirk and Mandisa																				
Open the Eyes of My Heart by Michael W. Smith																				
Smile/Better is One Day in Your Courts by Jonathan Nelson																				
Trust In You by Lauren Daigle																				

Confirmation Vocabulary

Recommended verses: See appendix
Difficulty: easy

Confirmation Day is coming. This year, you will be confirmed and become an adult in the church. Soon, your growth in faith and your relationship with God will become your sole responsibility. Before you are confirmed, you need to learn the definitions of the confirmation vocabulary. You decide to learn three words every day until all eighteen words are learned. Here are the vocabulary words:[43]

1. **Apostles.** "Twelve men Jesus had chosen to help him in his teaching."
2. **Ascension.** "Jesus's return to the father. Usually remembered with Jesus ascending into the sky."
3. **Baptism.** "Sacrament where God cleanses all sin and makes one a sharer in divine life, and a member of Christ's body, through the church."
4. **Communion.** "The [gathering] of Christian worship[ers] to participate in the Eucharist." [44]
5. **Confirmation.** "The rite when a baptized person affirms Christian belief and is admitted as a full member of the church."
6. **Crucifixion.** When Jesus dies on the cross and his soul descends to the dead. [45]
7. **Disciple.** A person "who learns from and follows Jesus Christ."
8. **Eucharist.** A sacrament where bread and wine become the body and blood of Jesus and are eaten.
9. **Faith.** "The strong belief in God or in the doctrines of a religion, based on spiritual apprehension rather than proof." [46]
10. **Grace (in Christian belief).** "The free and unmerited favor of God, as [shown] in the salvation of sinners and the [gift] of blessings."
11. **Holy Spirit.** "The third person in the Trinity." Jesus promises to send the Holy Spirit after his departure. [47]
12. **Incarnation.** "A Catholic teaching that the Son of God took on human flesh in the person of Jesus Christ."
13. **Jesus.** "The incarnation of God who is born of a virgin, crucified, died, and returned from the dead after three days. His death means that people who believe in him can be freed from sin. Jesus is also the second person in the Trinity. Also called 'the Son.'"
14. **Last Supper.** "The supper of Jesus with his disciples on the eve of his crucifixion." It occurred during the Jewish holiday called Passover.
15. **Reconciliation.** "Restoring peace and harmony to estranged parties. Jesus Christ brings peace and reconciliation by acting as a mediator between God and humanity."
16. **Resurrection**. "The body of Jesus rising from the dead, on the third day after his death on the cross and burial in the tomb. As a result, Christians have the hope of resurrection with Christ on the last day."
17. **Sacrament.** "A formal religious act conferring a specific grace on those who receive it."
18. **Sin.** "An offense against God." Also, an absence from God that feels like emptiness in a human being.

---

[43] "Vocab Part 6." Quizlet. Accessed August 6, 2016. https://quizlet.com/112908290/vocab-part-6-flash-cards/.

[44] Google Search. Accessed August 6, 2016. https://www.google.com/search

[45] Same as #43

[46] Same as #44

[47] Same as #43

The clues show which definitions you learn on which day.

Categories

Day (three words learned per day): 1, 2, 3, 4, 5, and 6

Definition: apostles, ascension, baptism, communion, confirmation, crucifixion, disciple, Eucharist, faith, grace, Holy Spirit, incarnation, Jesus, Last Supper, reconciliation, resurrection, sacrament, and sin

Clues

1. The definitions learned on day 1 are not for crucifixion, Holy Spirit, or sacrament.
2. The definitions learned on day 2 are not for apostles, disciple, faith, or sacrament.
3. The definitions learned on day 3 are not for baptism, crucifixion, Eucharist, Holy Spirit, or sin.
4. The definitions learned on day 4 are not for apostles, ascension, baptism, resurrection, or sin.
5. The definitions learned on day 5 are not for grace, Holy Spirit, incarnation, or Jesus.
6. The definitions learned on day 6 are not for ascension, communion, incarnation, or resurrection.
7. The definition of confirmation is learned on day 1, the definition of reconciliation is learned on day 4, and the definition of Last Supper is learned on day 5.
8. Communion, confirmation, and crucifixion are all learned on different days.
9. The definition of disciple is learned on the same day as grace but not on the same day as Last Supper.
10. Baptism, crucifixion, and sacrament are all learned on the same day.
11. The definition of Holy Spirit is learned after day 3.
12. The definition for disciple is learned two days after the definition for faith.
13. Consider the definitions for apostles, Eucharist, and resurrection: they are learned on day 1, day 2, and day 5.
14. The definition for Jesus is learned two or more days before the definition for apostles.
15. Consider the definitions for communion, Jesus, and sin: they are learned on days 2 and 5.
16. Resurrection is learned on the same day as communion.

Grid for Confirmation Vocabulary

	Apostles	Ascension	Baptism	Communion	Confirmation	Crucifixion	Disciple	Eucharist	Faith	Grace	Holy Spirit	Incarnation	Jesus	Last Supper	Reconciliation	Resurrection	Sacrament	Sin
Day 1																		
Day 1																		
Day 1																		
Day 2																		
Day 2																		
Day 2																		
Day 3																		
Day 3																		
Day 3																		
Day 4																		
Day 4																		
Day 4																		
Day 5																		
Day 5																		
Day 5																		
Day 6																		
Day 6																		
Day 6																		

Christmas Carols

Recommended verses: See appendix
Difficulty: hard

As December 25 nears, Christmas music is everywhere. It's played on the radio and seen on television. It is heard in malls, churches, and homes. Some people even go door-to-door Christmas caroling. Christmas songs are great; just remember why people sing. People sing to celebrate the memory of Jesus's birth and all the promises that are fulfilled with his life.

Thirteen Christians were asked about their favorite Christmas songs. Each of them listed one religious song and one secular song. Match the name of the Christian with the songs he or she mentioned.

Categories

Name: Adair, Bertha, Clyde, Danielle, Enzo, Gerry, Ishmael, Hope, Kwatoko, Marcy, Olivia, Solette, and Winona

Religious song: "Angels We Have Heard on High," "Away in a Manger," "Breath of Heaven," "Gaudete," "Go Tell It on the Mountain," "Joy to the World," "Little Drummer Boy," "Mary Had a Baby," "O Come, All Ye Faithful," "Silent Night," "The First Noel," "We Three Kings," and "What Child Is This?"

Secular song: "Deck the Halls," "Frosty the Snowman," "Grandma Got Run over by a Reindeer," "It's Beginning to Look a Lot Like Christmas," "Jingle Bell Rock," "Jingle Bells," "Must Be Santa," "O, Christmas Tree," "Rudolph the Red-Nosed Reindeer," "Santa Claus Is Coming to Town," "The Twelve Days of Christmas," "Up on a Housetop," and "Winter Wonderland"

Clues

1. The person who favored "The First Noel" also favored "It's Beginning to Look a Lot Like Christmas."
2. Marcy favored "Go Tell It on the Mountain," but not "Santa Claus Is Coming to Town."
3. "Rudolph the Red-Nosed Reindeer" was favored by Kwatoko or the person who favored "Away in a Manager."
4. Consider Clyde, Ishmael, and Solette: they favor the Christian songs "Angels We Have Heard on High" or "Gaudete" or the secular song "Must Be Santa."
5. "The First Noel" is favored by Enzo or Winona.
6. "Breath of Heaven" is favored by the person who likes "The Twelve Days of Christmas."
7. Adair, Bertha, Clyde, Danielle, Enzo, and Gerry do not favor "The Little Drummer Boy."
8. Hope, Ishmael, Kwatoko, Marcy, Olivia, Solette, and Winona do not favor "Silent Night."
9. The names of the people are as follows: Adair, Danielle, Hope, Ishmael, Solette; the people who like the Christian songs "Away in a Manger," "Breath of Heaven," "Little Drummer Boy," "Silent Night," and "We Three Kings"; and the people who like the secular songs "Deck the Halls," "It's Beginning to Look a Lot like Christmas," and "Jingle Bell Rock."
10. Gerry favors "Frosty the Snowman," and Olivia favors "Deck the Halls."
11. The person who favors "Mary Had a Baby" also favors "Winter Wonderland."
12. Consider Hope, Ishmael, and Winona: they favor "Gaudete," "Joy to the World," and "Little Drummer Boy."
13. "O Come All Ye Faithful" was not favored by Bertha or Solette.
14. Consider Adair, Clyde, and Ishmael: they like the songs "Must Be Santa," "O, Christmas Tree," and "Winter Wonderland."

15. "Up on a Housetop" is not favored by Bertha, Hope, or Winona, or the person who likes "Silent Night."

16. Clyde favors "We Three Kings," but Solette does not favor "Grandma Got Run over by a Reindeer" or "Jingle Bells."

17. "O Come All Ye Faithful" is paired with "Santa Claus Is Coming to Town."

18. "Joy to the World" is not favored by the same person who likes "Grandma Got Run over by a Reindeer."

Grid for Christmas Carols

	Angels We Have Heard on High	Away in a Manger	Breath of Heaven	Gaudete	Go Tell It on the Mountain	Joy to the World	Little Drummer Boy	Mary Had a Baby	O Come, All ye Faithful	Silent Night	The First Noel	We Three Kings	What Child is this?	Deck the Halls	Frosty the Snowman	Grandma Got Runover by a Reindeer	It's Beginning to Look a Lot Like Christmas	Jingle Bell Rock	Jingle Bells	Must be Santa	O' Christmas Tree	Rudolph the Red Nosed Reindeer	Santa Claus is Coming to Town	Twelve Days of Christmas	Up on a Housetop	Winter Wonderland
Adair																										
Bertha																										
Clyde																										
Danielle																										
Enzo																										
Gerry																										
Hope																										
Ishmael																										
Kwatoko																										
Marcy																										
Olivia																										
Solette																										
Winona																										
Deck the Halls																										
Frosty the Snowman																										
Grandma Got Runover by a Reindeer																										
It's Beginning to Look a Lot Like Christmas																										
Jingle Bell Rock																										
Jingle Bells																										
Must be Santa																										
O' Christmas Tree																										
Rudolph the Red Nosed Reindeer																										
Santa Claus is Coming to Town																										
Twelve Days of Christmas																										
Up on a Housetop																										
Winter Wonderland																										

Christmas Lists of Poor Families
Recommended verses: See appendix
Difficulty: medium

Christmas is coming, and your church has set out its Angel Tree. The Angel Tree is a tree outside the sanctuary. Here poor families will place paper angels on the tree. Each angel lists a few gifts that the family asks for because they cannot afford these gifts themselves. You are helping the church committee with the Angel Tree this year, so you know the identity of each family, but you know something more important too. You know about the secretly wanted gifts. Secretly wanted gifts are the things that poor people are often denied, though all humans are entitled to.

Match the family number with the gift the adult asked for, the gift the child asked for, and the secretly wanted gift.

Categories
Family number: 1, 2, 3, 4, 5, 6, 7, and 8
Adult gift: blanket, canned food, card table, coats, diapers, shoes, space heater, and toilet paper
Child gift: books, cards, dinosaur figures, doll, drawing pad, teddy bear, train, and video game
Secretly wanted gift: dignity, friendship, happiness. health, love, purpose, respect, and security

Clues
1. Friendship is the secretly wanted gift of the family that asked for a teddy bear.
2. The space heater and toilet paper were requested by families with an even number.
3. The family that asked for dinosaur figures also asked for toilet paper.
4. Family 1 secretly wants purpose, and family 6 secretly wants respect.
5. Consider the families who secretly want happiness, purpose, and security: they also requested a blanket, a card table, and coats.
6. The families are as follows: family 4, family 6, family 8, families with adults who requested a blanket and coats, and the families with the children that requested books, a drawing pad, and a teddy bear.
7. The family that secretly wants dignity also asked for books but is not family 3.
8. The family where the adult asked for a blanket has a child who asked for a video game.
9. Family 1 wants a card table, family 2 wants friendship, family 3 wants a doll, and family 4 wants love.
10. Consider families 5, 6, 7, and 8: they requested dignity, happiness, health, and respect. Also, one of them requested the space heater.
11. The family that requested a train also requested diapers, but it was not family #4.
12. Consider the families 2, 7, and 8: they requested a blanket, shoes, and a space heater.
13. The family that asked for cards did not ask for shoes

Grid for Christmas Lists of Poor Families

	Blanket	Canned Food	Card Table	Coats	Diapers	Shoes	Space Heater	Toilet Paper	Dignity	Friendship	Happiness	Health	Love	Purpose	Respect	Security	Books	Cards	Dinosaur Figures	Doll	Drawing Pad	Teddy Bear	Train	Video Game
Family #1																								
Family #2																								
Family #3																								
Family #4																								
Family #5																								
Family #6																								
Family #7																								
Family #8																								
Books																								
Cards																								
Dinosaur Figures																								
Doll																								
Drawing Pad																								
Teddy bear																								
Train																								
Video game																								
Dignity																								
Friendship																								
Happiness																								
Health																								
Love																								
Purpose																								
Respect																								
Security																								

Christmas Pageant

Recommended verses: See appendix
Difficulty: easy

Your church is having its annual Christmas pageant with the first and second graders. Match each kid's name with the part he or she is playing.

Categories

Name: Annabelle, Caitlin, D'Quan, Erica, Gavin, Harris, Ivan, Keitaro, Lucille, Marcos, Nikki, Ping, Tommy, and Wilbur

Part: Angel Gabriel, Angel 2, Angel 3, Innkeeper, Joseph, King Herod, Mary, Narrator, Shepherd 1, Shepherd 2, Shepherd 3, Wise Man 1, Wise Man 2, and Wise Man 3

Clues

1. If Gavin is Wise Man 2, then Catlin is Mary.
2. If Harris is Angel 3, then Nikki is Angel Gabriel.
3. Consider D'Quan, Keitaro, and Wilbur: they are playing King Herod, Wiseman 1, and Wise Man 3.
4. Gavin is not a shepherd, Harris is not Joseph, and Ping is not an angel.
5. Annabelle is Mary or the Narrator.
6. Erica is Angel 2 or Angel 3, Harris is the Narrator or Shepherd 1, Lucille is the Innkeeper or Mary, Marcos is Angel Gabriel or Wise Man 2.
7. The part of Joseph is played by Harris, Ivan, or Keitaro.
8. Ping is Angel 2, Shepherd 2, or Wise Man 2.
9. The shepherds are Harris, Ping, and Tommy.
10. The part of Mary is played by Catlin or Lucille.
11. Catlin and Gavin are not angels or the Innkeeper.
12. D'Quan is Wise Man 3, and Erica is Angel 2.
13. Wilbur is not Wise Man 1.

Grid for Christmas Pageant

	Angel Gabriel	Angel #2	Angel #3	Inn Keeper	Joseph	King Herod	Mary	Narrator	Shepherd #1	Shepherd #2	Shepherd #3	Wise Man #1	Wise Man #2	Wise Man #3
Annabelle														
Caitlin														
D'Quan														
Erica														
Gavin														
Harris														
Ivan														
Keitaro														
Lucile														
Marcos														
Nikki														
Ping														
Tommy														
Wilbur														

Appendix

Here are a few Bible verses based on the topics in *Christian Logic Puzzles*. Remember, every verse has a context that gives it meaning. Using a verse out of context can have dire consequences.

Animals: Genesis 1:20–31, Psalm 104:10–18
Armor of God: Ephesians 6:13–18
Babies: Isaiah 7:14, John 16:21, Psalm 139:13–16
Balaam's donkey: Numbers 22:21–39
Baptism: Matthew 3:13–17
Celebrations/Parties: Ecclesiastes 8:15
Christian roots: 1 Corinthians 3:6–9, Luke 11:33
Death: 1 Thessalonians 4:13–18
Disciples: John 1:35–50, Matthew 16:24–25
Enemies: Romans 12:19–20
Friends: 1 Corinthians 15:33
Fruit of the Spirit: Galatians 5:19–24
Future: Jeremiah 29:11, Philippians 1:6
Hard times: 2 Corinthians 4:8–9, Joshua 1:9, Psalm 40:1–17, Revelation 21:1–4
Jesus
- Birth: Luke 1:26–35, Matthew 1:18–2:23
- Crucifixion: John 19:1–6
- Death: Luke 23:26–46
- Lazarus: John 11:38–44
- Feeds five thousand: Mark 6:33–44
- Heals a blind man: John 9:1–41, Luke 18:35–43
- Heals a paraplegic man: Mark 2:1–12
- Removes demons: Luke 8:26–35
- Last Supper: Mark 14:18–24
- Palm Sunday: Matthew 21:1–11
- Resurrection: Luke 24:1–12, Matthew 28:1–10

Love: 1 Corinthians 13:1–13, 1 John 3:17, Luke 10:25–37
Mission trips: Isaiah 6:8, Matthew 28:19
Music: 2 Chronicles 5:12–14, 7, all of Psalms
Pastors: Acts 20:28, 1 Peter 5:1–4
Parables:
- Evil farmers: Matthew 21:33–46
- Farmer scattering seeds: Matthew 13:3–9
- Fishing net: Matthew 13:47–50
- Good Samarian: Luke 10:30–35
- Lost sheep: 1 Luke 15:4–7
- Ten bridesmaids: Matthew 25:1–13
- Three servants: Matthew 25:14–30
- Unforgiving debtor: Matthew 18:21–35

People

- Ahab: 1 Kings 16:29–34
- Anna: Luke 2:36–38
- Asa: 2 Chronicles 14-16
- Bathsheba: 2 Samuel 11:2–5
- Cyrus: Ezra 1:1–11
- David: 1 Samuel 17:45–49
- Deborah: Judges 4:4–14
- Elizabeth: Luke 1:36–45
- Esther: Any verses from the book of Esther
- Elijah: 1 Kings 17-19
- Eve: Genesis 2:21–3:6
- Gomer: Hosea 1:2–9
- Habakkuk: Any verses from the book of Habakkuk
- Haggai: Any verses from the book of Haggai
- Herod Agrippa: Matthew 14:1–12
- Hosea: Any verses from the book of Hosea
- Jacob: Genesis 25:19–35:15
- Jezebel: 1 Kings 21:5–15
- John the Baptist: Luke 1:5–25, Matthew 3:1–17, Matthew 14:1–14
- Lazarus: John 11:1–44
- Leah: Genesis 29:16–18, 31–35
- Lot's daughters: Genesis 19:33–38
- Lucius of Cyrene: Acts 11:19–20, Acts 13:1
- Lydia: Acts 16:14–15
- Martha: John 11:17–27
- Mary Magdalene: Luke 8:1–3
- Miriam: Exodus 2:1–10, 15:20–21
- Moses: Large portions of Exodus and Deuteronomy
- Naaman's wife's servant: 2 Kings 5:1–27
- Nahum: Any verses from the book of Nahum
- Nebuchadnezzar: Daniel 2:1–4:37
- Noah: Genesis 5:32–10:1
- Obadiah: Any verses from the book of Obadiah
- Paul (previously Saul): Acts 9:1–30, 12:25–28:31
- Pharaoh: See "Plagues"
- Philip the Evangelist: Acts 8:26–40
- Philip the Evangelist's daughters: Acts 21:8–9
- Priscilla: Romans 16:3–4
- Rahab: Joshua 2:1–20
- Rehoboam: 1 Kings 12:1–14
- Samaritan woman: John 4:1–29
- Samuel: Any verses from the book of 1 Samuel
- Sarah: Genesis 17:15–18:15, 21:1–6

- Saul (King): Any verses in 1 Samuel, starting at chapter 9
- Solomon: 1 Kings 3:10–28
- Queen of Sheba: 1 Kings 10:1–13
- Zephaniah: Any verses from the book of Zephaniah

Plagues: Exodus 7:14–11:10

Saints/Martyrs: Matthew 16:24–25, 24:9–14

Science: 1 Corinthians 10:31, Job 38:4–15, Proverbs 2:6

Teaching: 2 Timothy 3:16–17

Ten Commandments: Exodus 20:1–7

Trinity: John 1:1–5

Weddings: Ecclesiastes 4:12, Genesis 2:22–24

Wisdom: 1 Corinthians 1:26–29, Proverbs 1:1–7

Work: Colossians 3:23–24

Volunteering: Hebrews 6:10, Matthew 25:34–46, 1 Peter 4:10

Youth: 1 Corinthians 13:11, Ephesians 6:1–3, 1 Timothy 4:12

Works Cited

"Ambrose." Wikipedia. 2016. Accessed August 11, 2016. https://en.wikipedia.org/wiki/Ambrose. Miller, OFM Fr. Don. "Blessed Charles de Foucauld." Franciscan Media. Accessed August 11, 2016. https://www.franciscanmedia.org/blessed-charles-de-foucauld/

"Dictionary by Merriam-Webster: America's most-trusted online dictionary." Merriam-Webster. Accessed July 29, 2016. https://www.merriam-webster.com/.

Ehman, Mandi. "DIY Resurrection Eggs & Easter Story Book Printables." Life Your Way. Accessed April 2016.

"Esther John." Westminster Abbey ". 2016. Accessed August 10, 2016. http://www.westminster-abbey.org/our-history/people/esther-john.

"Fruit of the Spirit: Laminated Wall Chart." Rose Publishing, 2004. Accessed July 16, 2016.

Google Search. Accessed August 6, 2016. https://www.google.com/search

Isenhoff, Michelle. "Egyptian gods and the Ten Plagues." The Book and the Author. August 06, 2012. Accessed July 3, 2016. https://shellsstory.wordpress.com/2012/06/03/1821/.

"List of Christians in science and technology." Wikipedia. 2016. Accessed July 31, 2016. https://en.wikipedia.org/wiki/List_of_Christians_in_science_and_technology. "List of Christians in Science and Technology." *Wikipedia*. Wikimedia Foundation. Web. 31 July 2016.

Luker, Lamonte. "Survey of the Old Testament Class." Lutheran Theological Southern Seminary, Columbia, SC. Lecture. Fall 2014.

MacArthur, John. "The Believer's Armor: God's Provision for Your Protection." Grace To You. Accessed July 26, 2016.

Miller, OFM Fr. Don. "Blessed Charles de Foucauld." Franciscan Media. Accessed August 11, 2016. https://www.franciscanmedia.org/blessed-charles-de-foucauld/ Same as #16 Pages 66–67.

Miller, OFM Fr. Don. "Saint Josephine Bakhita." Franciscan Media. 2016. Accessed August 11, 2016. https://www.franciscanmedia.org/saint-josephine-bakhita/.

Miller, OFM Fr. Don. "St. Margaret of Cortona." Franciscan Media. 2016. Accessed August 11, 2016. https://www.franciscanmedia.org/saint-margaret-of-cortona/. AmericanCatholic.org. Web. 11 Aug. 2016.

Mulvihill, Margaret, and David Hugh. Farmer. The treasury of saints and martyrs. New York: Viking, 1999. Page 47

NIV Bible. London: Hodder & Stoughton Ltd, 2007.

Online, Catholic. "St. Gerard Majella - Saints & Angels." Catholic Online. 2016. Accessed August 10, 2016. http://www.catholic.org/saints/saint.php?saint_id=150.

"Perpetua." Christian History | Learn the History of Christianity & the Church. 2016. Accessed September 13, 2016. http://www.christianitytoday.com/history/people/martyrs/perpetua.html.

"Polycarp." Christian History | Learn the History of Christianity & the Church. 2016. Accessed September 13, 2016. http://www.christianitytoday.com/history/people/martyrs/perpetua.html.

"Saint Drogo." CatholicSaints.Info. May 12, 2016. Accessed August 9, 2016. https://catholicsaints.info/saint-drogo/.

"Spiritual Gifts Tests for Adult and Youth." Spiritual Gifts Test. Accessed July 27, 2016. https://spiritualgiftstest.com/

"St. Ambrose." CATHOLIC ENCYCLOPEDIA: St. Ambrose. 1905. Accessed August 11, 2016. http://www.newadvent.org/cathen/01383c.htm.

Trueman, C.N. "Nicholas Ridley." History Learning Site. 2016. Accessed September 07, 2016. http://www.historylearningsite.co.uk/tudor-england/nicholas-ridley/.

Tomkins, Stephen. "John Hus, Reforner Of Bohemia." Christian History Institute. Accessed August 03, 2016. https://www.christianhistoryinstitute.org/study/module/hus/.

"Vocab Part 6." Quizlet. Accessed August 6, 2016. https://quizlet.com/112908290/vocab-part-6-flash-cards/.

Answer Key

Engagement and Wedding Plans Key

Amber	Jesse	Waterfall	March	Violet
Becky	Robert	Bowling Alley	July	Pink
Emma	Blake	Street/Flash Mob	February	White
Gina	James	Park	January	Blue
Jamie	Tim	Church	August	Yellow
Lauren	Kyle	Beach	May	Silver
Natalie	Hunter	Fancy Restaurant	April	Red
Shana	TJ	Boat	June	Green

Choosing an Old Testament Story

Abby	Queen Esther	8
Ben	The Plagues of Egypt	2
Caden	Elijah the Prophet	6
Darla	Noah's Ark	4
Ernest	David and Goliath	10

Choosing a Story about Jesus

Clarissa	Parable of the Good Samaritan	8
Harry	Jesus Feeds Five Thousand	2
Logan	Jesus' Birth	6
Rose	Heals a man with demons	7
Simon	Resurrection	4
Yazmin	Brings Lazarus back to Life	5
Willow	Jesus' Death	1
Zola	Heals a Paralyzed man	3

Blessing of the Animals: Year 1

Brown	Stu	Rabbit
Davidson	Trixie	Hamster
Everett	Grace	Cat-Tabby
Irving	Lucky	Cat-Siamese
Peterson	Don	Exotic Fish
Reed	Mimi	Parrot
Vander	Fred	Dog- St. Bernard
Whitterson	Izzy	Dog-Yorkshire Terrier

Blessing of the Animals: Year 2

Angelou	Cameron	Dog-Great Dane
Crawford	Electra	Cat-Bengal
Eissler	Boomerang	Dog-Pomerian
Hanaway	Chloe	Fancy Rat
Lyon	Poe	Bird-Cockatoo
Mathus	Astrid	Cat-Ragdoll
Smith	Zinnia	Bird-Lovebird
Washington	Junnifer	Dog-American Staffordshire Terrier
West	Homer	Frog

Blessing of the Animals: Year 3

Brooks	Slinky	Cat-Sphynx
Davis	Vespera	Snake
Hale	Digger	Ferret
Ivory	Fox	Koi Fish
Lockhart	Ruby	Horse
Moore	Thursday	Dog-Border Collie
Noble	Macaroni	Dog-Staffordshire Bull Terrier
Pickens	Lightening	Cat-Persian
Urban	Yuri	Dog-Labrador Retriever

Global Mission Trips

Blessed Be	Japan	4 Weeks
Christ the King	Russia	2 Weeks
Cross and Crown	Kuwait	7 Weeks
Holy Trinity	South Africa	3 Weeks
Resurrection	Haiti	6 Weeks
Redeemer	Cuba	9 Weeks
St. Mark's	United States	5 Weeks
St. Mary's	Mexico	10 Weeks
St. Peter's	India	8 Weeks

Youth Volunteers

George	Differently-Abled Dance	Friend
Harriet	Soup'er Bowl	Parent
Megan	Fundraiser to cure Lupus	Grandparent
Patrick	Vacation Bible School	Teacher
Natasha	Thanksgiving Dinner for the Retirement Home	Nobody
Rachel	English as a Second Language Class	Pastor

Answer Key

Mission Trips in Africa

All Are Welcome	Gambia	9 Weeks
Community of Believers	Botswana	6 Weeks
International	Morocco	8 Weeks
Led by Faith	Zimbabwe	3 Weeks
Many Blesssings	Egypt	7 Weeks
Pine Valley	Angola	4 Weeks
Solid Rock	Sudan	5 Weeks

Mission Trips in Asia

Blessed Mary	China	8 Weeks
City of Faith	Myanmar	2 Weeks
Hill Top	Saudi Arabia	3 Weeks
Living Shepherd	Iran	5 Weeks
Mt. of Olives	Yemen	9 Weeks
New Hope	North Korea	7 Weeks
Serenity	Vietnam	6 Weeks
United	Thailand	4 Weeks

Mission Trips in Europe

Bethany	Italy	4 Weeks
Community of the	Germany	3 Weeks
Discipleship	France	6 Weeks
Grace	Iceland	9 Weeks
Mt. Hope	United Kingdom	8 weeks
Peace	Spain	2 Weeks
Southside	Sweden	5 Weeks
Woodland	Romania	7 Weeks

Mission Trips in South America

Celestial	Suriname	8 Weeks
Freedom	Ecuador	7 Weeks
Heavenly Father	Uruguay	2 Weeks
New Life	Chile	4 Weeks
Oasis	Brazil	9 Weeks
Pilgrim	Venezuela	3 Weeks
St. Matthew	Peru	5 Weeks
Zion	Argentina	6 Weeks

Mission Trips in the United States of America

All Nations	Michigan	5 Weeks
Church of God	New York	3 Weeks
First	Oregon	4 Weeks
Living Water	Kansas	7 Weeks
My Redeemer Lives	Texas	8 Weeks
New Jerusalem	South Carolina	9 Weeks
St. Luke's	California	6 Weeks
Way, Truth, and Life	Louisiana	2 Weeks

Armor of God

April	Pauline	Wooden Figure	Sword of the Spirit
Diamond	Isabelle	Aluminum Foil Figure	Belt of Truth
Jabari	Calvin	Colored-Pencil Sketch	Shield of Faith
Lavinia	Elizabeth	Painting	Shoes to Spread the Gospel of Peace
Tony	Gus	Metal Figure	Helmet of Salvation
William	Blaine	Magazine Collage	Breast Plate of Righteousness

Teaching the 10 Commandments

Avery	Keep the Sabbath Day Holy
Franklin	Honor Parents
Holly	No False Witnesses
Josephine	No Other Gods
Lola	No Idols
Malcolm	No Adultery
Odelia	No Coveting
Tanner	Don't Misuse God's Name
Vince	No Stealing
Zahra	No Killing

The Trinity: Father, Son and Holy Spirit

Arianna	Person	Relationship
Coby	Water	Essence
Michael	Finsihed Cake	Unity
Spencer	Three-Leaved Clover	Love

A Pastor's Day

8:00 AM	Prayer and silent mediation
10:00 AM	Visit sick and shut-ins
12:00 PM	Meet with congregants
2:00 PM	Read Bible
4:00 PM	Start writing sermon
6:00 PM	Attend Council meeting
8:00 PM	Reviewing notes for Thursday's funeral

Fruit of the Spirit

Week 1	Gentleness	Orson	Cherries
Week 2	Faithfulness	Ivan	Pears
Week 3	Joy	Fritz	Oranges
Week 4	Kindness	Heidi	Lemon
Week 5	Self-Control	Gwen	Watermelon
Week 6	Goodness	Marley	Bananas
Week 7	Forbearance	Zeke	Grapes
Week 8	Love	Russell	Pineapple
Week 9	Peace	Elle	Blueberries

Christan Lecture Series

101	Prof. Fjord	Parenting
102	Prof. Hill	Refugees
103	Prof. Knowlin	Money & Economics
104	Prof. Ratcliffe	Gay & Lesbian Marriage
105	Prof. Green	Women Preachers
106	Prof. Sterling	Relationships & Sex
107	Prof. White	Abortion
108	Prof. Mirse	Depression & Suicide
109	Prof. Calloway	Marriage & Divorce
110	Prof. Boyle	Evolution
111	Prof. Quentin	Evangelism
112	Prof. Price	The Death Penalty

Seminary Class Schedule

Church History	Prof. Gutiérrez	Thursday	6	Advice #11
Diaconal Ministry	Prof. Swinton	Monday	3	Advice #7
Ethics	Prof.Overett	Wednesday	3	Advice #2
Greek	Prof. Miller	Tuesday	4	Advice #1
Hebrew	Prof. Cena	Monday	2	Advice #9
New Testament	Prof. Paris	Thursday	5	Advice #12
Old Testament	Prof. DiCamillo	Tuesday	4	Advice #3
Pastoral Care	Prof. Winters	Tuesday	5	Advice #6
Preaching	Prof. Keller	Wednesday	7	Advice #4
Sacraments	Prof. Albom	Monday	2	Advice #5
Teaching	Prof. Hyland	Thursday	6	Advice #10
Theology	Prof. Thornton	Wednesday	7	Advice #8

Resurrection Eggs

Armand	Brown	Thimble
Blossom	Silver	Broken Toothpick
Cassie	Gold	Twig Crown
Doug	Pink	Rock
Ethan	Green	Piece of Leather
Giselle	Red	Paper Scroll
Keadra	Yellow	Soft Fabric
Malachi	Purple	Nothing
Roger	White	Dimes
Sybil	Orange	Leaf
Vadness	Blue	Nails
Xavier	Black	Dice

Hard times

Alice	Infertility	Talking with a Friend
Bane	Dying Marriage	Creating Art
Charlotte	Joblessness	Reading Bible
Elliot	Cancer	Observing Nature
Gwen	Poverty	Volunteering
Kate	Single and Lonely	Quoting Scriptures
Louis	Death of a Family Member	Prayer and Mourning
Malika	Family Member with Dementia	Seeking Pastor's Guidance
Oliver	Going to Prison	Communion
Steve	Paralyzed	Attending Support Group
Vito	Homelessness	Singing Hymns
Yuki	Discrimination	Fasting

Easter Egg Hunt

Pre K-Kindergarten	425	Nursery	Mr. Piper
1st Grade	375	Sunday School room	Miss. Zander
2nd Grade	350	Front yard	Mr. Fry
3rd Grade	400	Playground	Miss. Dahl
4th Grade	300	Fellowship Hall	Mrs. Gardner
5th Grade	325	Backyard	Mr. Turner

Hard Times: High School Edition

Casey	Unsure about future career	Taking a spiritual gifts test	Jeremiah 29:11
Felicia	Bullied at school	Attending youth group	Romans 12:19-20
Hermione	Moving	Silent Meditation	Joshua 1:9
Jévon	Worried about college	Talking with a friend	Philippians 4:6-7
Ken	Failing classes	Meeting with a tutor	2 Corinthians 1:3-4
Lana	Peer-pressure to drink	Speaking with a counselor	1 Corinthians 15:33
Monique	Believes he/she is ugly	Journaling	1 Peter 3:3-4
Nino	Grandparent died	Playing with the dog	1 Thessalonians 4:13-18
Olivia	Eating disorder	Going to a doctor	1 Corinthians 6:19-20
Preston	Depression	Attending a support group	Psalm 40:1-3
Roxanne	Fighting with parents	Prayer	Romans 13:7
Scarlet	New stepparent	Playing an instrument	Ephesians 6:1–3
Tyrelle	End of relationship	Reading Bible	Psalm 147:3
Wally	Autistic	Being a Math tutor	1 Corinthians 1:26-29

My Soul Sings to You

Alejandro	On Eagle's Wings	Unbreakable by Fireflight
Claire	I am the Bread of Life	Forgiveness by Toby Mac
Jules	Nearer my God to Me	Overcomer by Mandisa
Latoya	Blessed Assurance	The Basin and the Towel by Michael Card
Marvin	Were You There...	Courageous by Casting Crowns
Perry	America the Beautiful	God's Not Dead by Newboys
Sable	Onward Christian Soldiers	Something about the Name Jesus by Kirk Franklin
Theodore	All are Welcome	Awesome God by Rich Mullins
Victoria	Jesus loves Me	My Soul will Rest by KMP Christian Celtic Band
Walter	Away in a Manger	Amazing Grace (My Chains are Gone) by Chris Tomlin

Spiritual Gifts: Romans 12:6-8

Exhortation	4
Giving	7
Leadership	9
Mercy	6
Prophecy	2
Serving	5
Teaching	11

Spiritual Gifts: 1 Corinthians 12:7-10

Distinguishing Between Spirits	Yvette
Faith	Henry
Healings	Zelda
Interpretation of Tongues	Richard
Miracles	Josh
Prophecy	Crystal
Tongues	Sarah
Word of Knowledge	Brandon
Word of Wisdom	Iesha

The Nine Soloists

Axel	Trombone	Ode to Joy
Dazhawn	Guitar	It is Well with my Soul
Helen	Violin	Take my Life, That I May Be
Jericho	Piano	Here I am Lord
Lafyette	Flute	One Bread, One Body
Madison	Bells	Jesus Remember Me
Nina	Trumpet	The Storm is Passing Over
Otto	Clarinet	How Great Thou Art
Silver	Saxaphone	Shout to the Lord

Spiritual Gifts: 1 Corinthians 12:28

Autumn	Teacher	Co-Worker
Coral	Kinds of healings	Teammate
Eddie	Prophet	Friend
Jeremy	Helps	Father
Lester	Miracles	Grandma
Misty	Apostleship	Mailman
Stormie	Tongues	Bus driver
Wayne	Administration	Neighbor

Christians Taking an Evolution Course

Dennis	Reason 2
Jasmine	Reason 1
Lex	Reason 4
Mario	Reason 3
Rose	Reason 5

Christian Men at Work

Alex	Marriage Counselor	Fishing
Buck	Waiter	Gardening
Dwayne	Anthropologist	Playing hockey
Forest	Dad working at home	Volunteering
Harrison	Genealogist	Watching crime shows
Jay	Translator	Weight-lifting
Kordell	Certified Nursing Assistant	Reading
Labron	Bookkeeper	Printmaking
Octavian	Fork Lift Driver	Cooking
Ronald	Illustrator	Jogging
Stephen	Painter	Traveling
Ulrich	Police Officer	Playing with the grandkids

Women of the Bible Presentations: Day 1

Anna	Fifi	B-
Elizabeth	Ulysses	B+
Esther	Charity	A-
Jezebel	Maria	B
Leah	Gwenelle	A
Lot's Daughters	Tau	C
Martha	Jordan	D
Mary	Harper	C+
Priscilla	Sid	F
Sarah	Darius	C-

Christian Women at Work

Brooklyn	Pharmacist	Social networking
Chaunsee	Jewelry Designer	Doll-making
Darcy	Paralegal	Watching football
Eve	Marketing Strategist	Making videos
Florette	Screenwriter	Bowling
Hadassah	Accountant	Swimming
Jewel	Ophthalmologist	Throwing parties
Myat	Graphic Designer	Zumba
Nicole	Mom working at home	Stargazing
Opal	End-of-life Counselor	Playing video games
Renee	Clown	Skydiving
Sylvia	Military Chaplain	Drawing Manga

Women of the Bible Presentations: Day 2

Bathsheba	Horatio	F
Deborah	Omar	A
Eve	Cheryl	D
Gomer	Stanley	B+
Lydia	Precious	B-
Miriam	Tod	C-
Mary Magdalene	Bonita	A-
Rahab	Wren	C+
Samaritan woman	Jillian	C
Ruth	Ace	B

Parables by Jesus

Blair	The Three Servants	5
Hailey	The Ten Bridesmaids	3
Rhianna	The Farmer Scattering Seeds	7
Scott	The Unforgiving Debtor	1
Takao	The Lost Sheep	6
Ursula	The Evil Farmers	2
Violet	The Fishing Net	4

More Saints and Martyrs

Arlene	Margaret of Cortona
Clark	Josephine Bakhita
Desmond	Charles De Foucauld
Kathleen	Francis Xavier
Fritz	Nicholas of Myra
Pennelope	Ambrose of Milan
Olander	Our Lady of Guadalupe
Ubon	Thomas Beckett
Yolanda	Veronica Giuliani

Saints and Martyrs

Candace	Nicholas Ridley
Fern	Polycarp of Smyrna
Havana	Jan Hus
Isadore	Perpetua
Jessica	Óscar Arnulfo Romero y Galdámez
Mikey	Elizabeth of Hungary
Shawn	Joan of Arc
Turquoise	Drogo
Wilson	Gerard Majella
Xun	Esther Jonh

The Plagues of Egypt

Blood	Naomi
Darkness	Joyce
Death of the Firstborn Son	Maureen
Festering Boils	Zane
Flies	Billy
Frogs	Walter
Gnats	Vyra
Hail	Dominique
Livestock	Sylvester
Locusts	Pamela

Happy Birthday Baby!

January	Titus	Wednesday	12:37 PM
February	Jenny	Tuesday	6:05 PM
March	Xander	Saturday	5:02 AM
April	Belle	Monday	3:09 AM
May	Faith	Thursday	2:45 AM
June	Issac	Tuesday	1:15 PM
July	Elmyra	Friday	7:13 PM
August	Milo	Wednesday	12:07 AM
September	Uma	Thursday	9:55 PM
October	Rufus	Friday	11:24 AM
November	Gerald	Monday	8:38 AM
December	Océane	Sunday	4:36 PM

Nineteen Ways to Describe God

Biggest thing out there	Isaiah 66:1
Faithful	1 Corinthians 10:13
Father	1 Corinthians 8:6
Impartial	Deuteronomy 10:17
Jealous	Deuteronomy 4:23-24
Judge	Psalm 76:7-10
King of the Earth	Psalm 47:7
Lion	Hosea 11:10
Love	1 John 4:16
Merciful	Ephesians 2:4-5
Mother	Isaiah 66:13
Mysterious	Job 11:7-9
Omnipotent	Revelation 19:6
Omnipresent	Psalms 139:7 – 18
Omniscient	Romans 11: 33-35
Prefect	Psalm 18:30
Protector of orphans and widows	Psalm 68:5
Righteous	Deuteronomy 32:4
Rock	Isaiah 26:4-5

Answer Key

Prophetic Books of the Bible

Angelica	Jonah	Daniel
Bennett	Micah	Isaiah
Connie	Amos	Jeremiah
Donald	Obadiah	Ezekiel
Hugo	Haggai	Jeremiah
Irma	Joel	Jeremiah
Judy	Nahum	Ezekiel
Mystelle	Zechariah	Isaiah
Rusty	Malachi	Lamentations
Satoshi	Habakkuk	Daniel
Tyrone	Hosea	Lamentations
Vivian	Zephaniah	Ezekiel

Baptisms

Brogan	8 months	3	Main Street
Elodie	5 years old	8	Lakeside
Ivy	29 years old	2	Community of the Cross
Gary	15 years old	4	First Assembly
Marita	38 years old	10	Second Coming
Hayden	40 years old	7	Good Samaritan
Raine	78 years old	16	Anointed
Sakura	62 years old	1	Calvary
Quint	2 months	5	Back to the Bible
Terrance	10 years old	12	Trinity

Jesus' Original 12 Disciples

Adele	Jude (Thaddeus)
Cole	James (the Elder)
D'Ante	Matthew (Levi)
Gordon	Peter (Simon Peter)
Hubert	Philip
Jim	Judas
Luther	Bartholomew (Nathanael)
Max	Simon (the Zealot)
Roark	Andrew
Teagan	James (the Younger)
Valmont	Thomas
Wade	John

Depression and Hope

Day 1	Ecclesiastes 9:4
Day 2	Psalm 43:5
Day 3	Psalm 34:18
Day 4	Philippians 4:6-8
Day 5	Psalm 42:11
Day 6	Matthew 5:3
Day 7	Proverbs 3:5-6
Day 8	Deuteronomy 31:8
Day 9	Philippians 13
Day 10	Deuteronomy 32:10
Day 11	Psalm 40:1-3
Day 12	John 3:16-17

Party Time

Bart	College Acceptance Party	14-May
Dustin	Bachelor Party	3-May
Gigi	Bachelorette Party	11-May
Hannah	Themed-Party	7-May
Jamar	Housewarming Party	5-May
Koji	Birthday Party	10-May
Reno	Wine Tasting Party	31-May
Stephanie	Game Night Party	26-May
Tamara	Graduation Party	25-May
Zamari	Dinner Party	18-May

To Be Loved and To Love

Brock	Matthew 5:43-48	#5
Chin-Hwa	Romans 8:37-39	#1
Herberto	John 15:13	#9
Jojo	John 13:34-35	#6
Kyran	1 John 4:9-12	#8
Marty	1 Corinthians 13:1-13	#3
Nadia	Mark 12:29-31	#7
Shelby	1 John 4:19-21	#2
Warren	Psalm 91:14-16	#4

Christian Roots

Andrés	Whole Foods
Brin	Harvard
Christopher	YMCA
Daichi	Hobby Lobby
Elba	Fellowship Travel International
Hildegarde	Divine Image Cosmetics
Ivette	Forever 21
Joy	George Foreman
Krysanthe	Bethel University
Lee	Lord's Gym
Marshal	Chick-Fil-A
Oprah	Interstate Batteries
Pablo	Tyson Foods
Stephanie	E Harmony
Tabitha	Habitat for Humanity
Victor	In-N-Out Burger
Wendell	Thrivent Financial
Yara	ServiceMaster

Kings and Queens

2	Nebuchnezzar	Adam	June
4	Asa	Pearl	Bella
6	Solomon	Hasan	Travone
8	Queen of Sheba	Kiki	Cynthia
10	Saul	Vladimir	Lief
12	Pharaoh	Gabby	Ming
14	Vashti	Freddie	Stella
16	Herod Agrippa	Tahoma	Joseph
18	Cyrus	Chris	Angel
20	Rehoboam	Barry	Drake
22	Ahab	Margaret	Roscoe
24	Esther	J'waun	Humphrey

How to be Beautiful

Amity	1 Samuel 16:7	Green
Chona	Ecclesiastes 3:11	Yellow
Ginger	1 Timothy 4:8	Brown
Heather	Psalm 139:13-16	Maroon
Kimiko	Proverbs 31:30	Black
Marissa	Genesis 1:27	Teal
Savannah	1 Peter 3:3-4	White
Zibiah	John 7:24	Pink

Christian Scientists Born Before 1700

Anton Maria of Rheita	4
Blaise Pascal	7
Francis Bacon	5
Isaac Barrow	8
Isaac Newton	7
Nicholas of Cusa	6
Nicole Oresme	6
Pierre Gassendi	5
Robert Boyle	8
William Turner	4

Christian Scientists Born 1700-1900

Group A	Marshall Hall	James David Forbes
Group B	Albrecht von Haller	Johannes Reinke
Group C	John Bachman	Charles Doolittle Walcott
Group D	George Washington Carver	Mary Anning
Group E	Charles Glover Barkla	Antoine Lavoisier

Answer Key

Christian Scientists Born in the 1900's

Greek Scholars	Charles H. Townes	Buzz	400	Incorrect
Greek Scholars	Kathleen Lonsdale	Hazel	100	Correct
Greek Scholars	Mary Celine Fasenmyer	Fabian	300	Incorrect
Greek Scholars	Joseph Murray	Travis	300	Correct
Greek Scholars	Stanley Jaki	Kalifa	500	Correct
Theo-tists	C. F. von Weizsäcker	Elenore	100	Incorrect
Theo-tists	George R. Price	Aurora	200	Incorrect
Theo-tists	Jérôme Lejeune	Monty	200	Incorrect
Theo-tists	Sir Robert Boyd	Penny	500	Correct
Theo-tists	Wernher von Braun	Conan	400	Correct

Prophets and Prophetesses Vol. 1

Akito	Obadiah
Evan	Philip the Evangelist
Hernán	Deborah
Jade	Nahum
Nakita	Hosea
Shanice	Lucius of Cyrene
Tobias	Habakkuk
Yasmina	Miriam

Prophets and Prophetesses Vol. 2

Bob	Zephaniah
Daffodil	John the Baptist
Fumiko	Elijah
Gregory	Haggai
Hironobu	Anna
Marina	Paul the Apostle
Octavia	The four daughters of Philip the Evangelist
Wendy	Moses

God Used Them

Anika	Samuel	Blind Man	B+
Emilio	Rahab	Peter	A
Herman	Moses	Lazarus	A-
Kyla	Sarah	Balaam's Donkey	B
Lance	Jacob	John the Baptist	C-
Maylene	Leah	Samaritan woman	C+
Phineas	Saul	Naaman's wife's servant	B-
Whitney	Noah	Demon Possessed Man	C

God Can Use You Too

Anton	Unemployed	Tuesday
Clay	Janitor	Wednesday
Devin	Atheist	Wednesday
Ginevra	Healthy	Monday
Heidi	Wheelchair Bound	Thursday
Jackie	Alcoholic	Monday
Kyoto	Parkinson's Disease	Tuesday
Laqueta	Wealthy	Friday
Maebelle	Celebrity	Saturday
Otis	College Graduate	Monday
Paul	Prisoner	Saturday
Rin	Introvert	Friday
Saddie	4th Grade Education	Sunday
Sherece	Married	Sunday
Theo	Newborn	Thursday
Uri	Dying	Sunday

Family Day at the Zoo

Abrams	Lion	Grilled Cheese	2
Elder	Penguin	Popcorn	1
Hamilton	Gorilla	Ice Cream	4
Jurgensen	Koala	Pizza	5
Lenoir	Sea Lion	Pretzel	3
Marsh	Snow Leopard	Corn Cob	4
Ortberg	Tiger	Cotton Candy	3
Quigg	Polar Bear	Burger	6
Reeves	Giraffe	Hot Dog	5
Sanders	African Elephant	Chicken Nuggets	4
Tally	Flamingo	Snow Cone	5
Yanos	Galápagos Tortoise	Salad	7

Volunteering in the Community		
Alastair	Medical Clinic	24
Bellissa	Retirement Home	8
Chieko	High School	16
Flannery	Community Center	10
Huey	Middle School	22
Jonathan	Animal Shelter	6
Katrine	Museum	20
May	Veteran Services Center	18
Niles	Homeless Shelter	2
Pearlina	Refugee Center	12
Susan	Disaster Relief Team	4
Taj	Day Care	14

John 3:16-17	
Ashley	Part 4
Hasina	Part 2
Jamal	Part 1
Lita	Part 5
Tom	Part 3

The Lord's Prayer		
Anna-Marie	Part 4	3rd
Nathan	Part 6	6th
Pedro	Part 1	2nd
Rebecca	Part 5	4th
Stan	Part 3	5th
Uma	Part 2	1st

Reacting to Violence and Hate	
Ambrose	Matthew 18:15-17
Corbin	Matthew 5:23-26
Dawn	Acts 17:26
Eli	Ephesians 6:10-18
Hank	Luke 18:1-8
Jane	James 2:14-2:26
Kalim	Galatians 3: 28-29
Lindsey	James 2:1-13
Payton	Luke 10:25-37
Rosaleen	2 Corinthians 5:18-21
Seanna	Psalm 11:5
Viola	Job 2:11-13

Confirmation Vocabulary	
Day 1	Eucharist
Day 1	Confirmation
Day 1	Faith
Day 2	Communion
Day 2	Jesus
Day 2	Resurrection
Day 3	Disciple
Day 3	Ascension
Day 3	Grace
Day 4	Incarnation
Day 4	Reconciliation
Day 4	Holy Spirit
Day 5	Sin
Day 5	Apostles
Day 5	Last Supper
Day 6	Baptism
Day 6	Crucifixion
Day 6	Sacrament

My Soul is Still Singing		
Bruno	What a Friend We Have in Jesus	Open the Eyes of My Heart by Michael W. Smith
Carmen	Gather Us In	Beyond the Moon and Stars by Dan Schutte
Hakeen	Battle Hymn of the Republic	Lord I Lift Your Name on High by Hill Song
Isabeau	Lift High the Cross	Smile/Better is One Day in Your Courts by Jonathan Nelson
Kelvin	A Might Fortress is Our God	Be One by Natalie Grant
Maggie	Amazing Grace	Jesus Take the Wheel by Carrie Underwood
Phoebe	Psalm 141-Let My Prayer Rise Up	Cry to Jesus by Third Day
Quigley	The Light of That City	Trust In You by Lauren Daigle
Tanishia	Let There Be Peace on Earth	God Bless America by The Gaither Vocal Band
Zoe	My Hope is Built on Nothing Less	Lose My Soul by Toby Mac, featuring Franklin Kirk and Mandisa

Answer Key

Christmas Carols		
Adair	Mary Had a Baby	Winter Wonderland
Bertha	Away in a Manger	Rudolph the Red Nosed Reindeer
Clyde	We Three Kings	Must be Santa
Danielle	O Come, All ye Faithful	Santa Claus is Coming to Town
Enzo	The First Noel	It's Beginning to Look a Lot Like Christmas
Gerry	Silent Night	Frosty the Snowman
Hope	Joy to the World	Jingle Bells
Ishmael	Gaudete	O' Christmas Tree
Kwatoko	Breath of Heaven	Twelve Days of Christmas
Marcy	Go Tell It on the Mountain	Jingle Bell Rock
Olivia	What Child is this?	Deck the Halls
Solette	Angels We Have Heard on High	Up on a Housetop
Winona	Little Drummer Boy	Grandma Got Run Over by a Reindeer

Chrsitmas Lists of Poor Families			
Family #1	Card Table	Drawing Pad	Purpose
Family #2	Shoes	Teddy Bear	Friendship
Family #3	Coats	Doll	Security
Family #4	Toilet Paper	Dinosaur Figures	Love
Family #5	Canned Food	Books	Dignity
Family #6	Diapers	Train	Respect
Family #7	Blanket	Video Game	Happiness
Family #8	Space Heater	Cards	Health

Christmas Pageant	
Annabelle	Narrator
Caitlin	Mary
D'Quan	Wise Man #3
Erica	Angel #2
Gavin	Wise Man #2
Harris	Shepherd #1
Ivan	Joseph
Keitaro	Wise Man #1
Lucile	Inn Keeper
Marcos	Angel Gabriel
Nikki	Angel #3
Ping	Shepherd #2
Tommy	Shepherd #3
Wilbur	King Herod

About the Author

Heather Marie Walker was born in Minnesota as a quiet child with a vivid imagination and the rare ability to read in a room full of screaming children. She grew up in White Bear Lake, but later moved to Goose Creek, South Carolina. In 2013, she graduated from Columbia College with a Bachelor's in Religion and English Literature. She further studied at the Lutheran Theological Southern Seminary. Her greatest accomplishments are receiving the 2014 United Way Community Impact Award, saving up $8,000 to buy her first car, and teaching her cat to sit.